FILLET OF PLACE

*The Parish Church of St Mary the Virgin, East Knoyle.*

# Fillet of Place

## *More Memories around East Knoyle*

ANTHONY CLAYDON

*For Joan*

First published in the United Kingdom in 2008 for the author by
The Hobnob Press, PO Box 1838, East Knoyle, Salisbury SP3 6FA
© Anthony Claydon

British Library Cataloguing in Publication Data
A catalogue record for this book is available from the British Library.

ISBN    978-0-946418-66-4
Typeset in 10.5/13 pt Georgia; typesetting and origination by John Chandler
Printed in Great Britain by Salisbury Printing Company Ltd, Salisbury

# Contents

*'Close ta ower leetle village church,*
*Under a girt big yew;*
*Who's spredden yarms da shelter graves,*
*Of sleepers not a vew.'*

Edward Slow of Wilton, *Wiltshire Rhymes.*

# Introduction and Acknowledgements

A S IN A PREVIOUS VOLUME about this part of South West Wiltshire,* I have used the term 'Knoyle' to apply specifically to East Knoyle, without intending any disrespesct towards the equally ancient twin village of West Knoyle, whose boundaries were described in a Royal Charter dated AD 948.

In a number of cases, the chapter Notes have named those who have made a special contribution. There are, however, many more people who have provided a wealth of information, advice and encouragement. They know who they are, and I would ask them all to accept my grateful thanks.

I would wish to thank Dr John Chandler of Hobnob Press for his unfailing support and wise guidance, and finally my wife Joan. Her constant encouragement and practical help have made this book possible.

The cover illustration is a detail from Robert Morden's 1695 Map of Wiltshire (reproduced by kind permission of Mrs. Elizabeth Halsall).

* *The Nature of Knoyle: East Knoyle, the people and the place* (Hobnob Press 2002)

# Castle Rings

Having subdued Gaul across the Channel, Julius Caesar's two campaigns against the Britons in 55 and 54 BC were the first indications that Rome might seek to expand the increasing trade links with British tribes into full political and military control. Some of the trappings of Roman civilization such as wines, silver and copperware were becoming common imports into the south east of Britain. These were paid for with cattle, leather hides, gold, silver, tin and slaves- captured during the endemic intertribal warfare. The Romans were past masters of the art of 'Divide and Rule' favouring one tribe against another in the expectation of securing a pro-Roman ally or client state.

Some of the tribes, such as the Atrebates, originally from Gaul but in the first century widely established across modern Surrey, Sussex and Hampshire, even adopted the style of 'Rex' ('King') on their coinage; while the Romans waited and watched – the old rhyme 'Will you come into my parlour, said the spider to the fly' comes to mind.

The inhabitants of Dorset, and for some distance to the north into Wiltshire, including Knoyle, were known as the Durotriges. They were the most westerly tribe to use coinage but had no specifically defined capital. Their coinage, like that of many other Celtic tribes was derived from that of Philip of Macedon, Alexander the Great's father, and depicted a horse and chariot. By the start of the 1st Century A.D. this had become almost indecipherable, though wheels were prominent and a disjointed horse was an important feature- possibly because one of the principal Celtic Gods was Epona the Horse. Although a head with a laurel wreath was discernible on the obverse side, there would be no identification of a ruler by name – which suggests that the Durotriges were a loose confederation, led by local chieftains. Based on evidence from other Celtic tribes, there was likely to

*A Stater coin of the Durotriges tribe, found in East Knoyle. It is dated between B.C. 60 and A.D. 20.*

have been a tribal council, capable of co-ordinating action when the need arose. Certainly there was a fierce spirit of independence, a willingness to trade but a reluctance to be sucked into political dependence on Rome.

Most people were peasant farmers, though there were craftsmen, traders and fishermen also. The tribal area contained over three dozen hillforts, ranging in size and importance from great centres like Maiden Castle, Hod Hill and Badbury Rings, to smaller locations serving just the local area. The nearest of these to East Knoyle was Castle Rings south of Semley.

To return to the Romans: For quite a while there was no hostile action from them, although the first Emperor, Augustus, is reckoned to have planned to invade on at least three occasions. After Augustus came the Emperor Tiberius and then Gaius – known as 'Caligula' 'Little Boot' from his love as a small boy of wearing a miniature soldier's uniform – the Caliga was a sort of half boot worn by the common soldiers. He was a hot tempered young man, also a schizophrenic and at the age of 28 assembled a force and ordered the invasion of Britain. Some of the troops refused, so the Emperor in disgust ordered them to go home loaded up with sea shells from the Channel shore as 'spoils of war'.

One year later Caligula was murdered by his official protectors, the Praetorian Guard, and Claudius succeeded him. Despised by the 'great and the good' Claudius determined to make his mark on history, sensing that a conquest of Britain would gain him prestige politically and impress the army.

He chose to despatch four legions stationed on the Rhine, many of whose members had become used to a settled existence there in comfortable circumstances.

It was at this time that the future Emperor Vespasian became a major player, particularly for Southern Britain. He was born at Falacrina near Sabine Reate in modern Switzerland. His father was Titus Flavinius Sabinus a successful tax collector turned banker of knighthood ('Equestrian') status, as was Vespasia Polla his wife.

His early years were spent with his parents being away on business for long periods, so that his education was largely entrusted to his grandmother. At the age of about 16, he was earmarked for a career in the Senate, including a spell on military duty in Thrace.

When Claudius became Emperor after Caligula's assassination, Vespasian's advancement was rapid. Although the new emperor was physically handicapped and not a very likeable personality, he was nevertheless nobody's fool. He rescued administration of the ship of state from its worst excesses under his predecessor, which had threatened to run it aground. He was widely read and while perhaps over keen on utilising Freedmen in high office, recognised ability when he saw it. With the assistance of the Emperor's freedman Narcissus,

*Vespasian, who was the fourth Emperor elected in the year A.D. 69. At the beginning of A.D. 43 he was Legate of the II Legion (Augusta), stationed at Strasbourg.*

Vespasian was appointed Legatus Legionis II Augustae (Legate of the Second Legion (Augusta)) stationed at Strasbourg. His first task was to plan the invasion of Britain. The other three Rhine legions assembled for the assault were IX Hispana, XIV Gemina and XX Valeria Victrix. All were unenthusiastic at the prospect of being uprooted and sent off to conduct a campaign in the northern fastnesses across the Channel.

On the northern Gaulish beaches the overall commander Aulus Plautius, a respected senator, faced a mutiny from his troops. Narcissus, the freedman and former slave, addressed them and won them over – it seems that his ability in rising from slavery to high office as the Emperor's secretary had earned their respect.

The landing was made in three divisions, with Legion II most probably setting out from Boulogne and landing at Lympne. Vespasian personally distinguished himself in a fierce two day battle reckoned to be near Rochester on the River Medway. Aulus Plautius then sent word to Claudius to cross the Channel and take command. A sixteen day visit, accompanied by reinforcements including camels and elephants, was (according to the historian Suetonius) sufficient for the Emperor to receive the submission of eleven kings. After a victory parade at Colchester, he returned to Rome to celebrate a Triumph in the following year. In fairness, it should be mentioned that although his physical infirmities had ruled out an active military career, he was extremely knowledgeable on military matters, and his military 'street credibility' now became established.

Vespasian took his legion to the Isle of Wight, conquered it, crossed over to the mainland at Hamworthy and set up winter quarters at what is now Lake Farm near Wimborne.

It is not clear exactly when Vespasian embarked on his task of subduing the Durotriges, but it is recorded that his campaign required the taking of twenty 'towns'. Some of these were major concentrations like Maiden Castle, Hambledon, Badbury Rings and Hod Hill, others would have been minor hillforts. With these neutralised, he seems to have conducted a sweep westward from Old Sarum, when one of the hillforts in his way would have been Castle Rings in Semley.

It was built in the Iron Age, possibly around BC 400, and consisted of a twelve acre area surrounded by a rampart and ditch. The site was investigated in 1912 and is Wiltshire Antiquity No. A.M 55. The remains of two original entrances survive half way up the eastern and western sides, while the height from the bottom of the ditch to the top of the rampart is still over four metres in places. The sides may have been revetted with wooden planking and the ramparts could have been topped with stakes. Since the defenders had worked out that the lie of the land made an attack from the east unlikely; they had created a second rampart 150 metres to the west, now ploughed out except in the area of Crates Wood. Until or unless overrun, this rampart would have had the advantage of unsighting the attackers.

There is no specific record of the attack on Castle Rings. However, Vespasian as Legion commander, no doubt in consultation with his brother who was Second

*A rampart and ditch of the 12 acre*     *The Western outer rampart of the Castle*
*Iron Age fort at Castle Rings, Semley.*          *Rings fort, at Crates Wood.*

in Command, and with the Praefectus Castrorum or Camp Prefect (responsible for logistical support) developed an effective method of attack against British hillforts. This last officer was Publius Anicius Maximus and a man of exceptional ability. He was to be decorated by the Emperor with awards of the Mural Crown and Unsullied Spear for his part in 'The British War' as recorded on a memorial stone erected at his birthplace now known as Yalvac, 140 miles southwest of Ankara by the City authorities of Alexandria in Egypt across the other side of the Mediterranean. His duties included provision and maintenance of the 'engines of war' including the Legion's 'Ballistae'. These were a type of catapult using torsion springs made of animal sinew which could deliver lethal iron bolts with great accuracy over a range of several hundred yards.

The attack on Castle Rings would have begun with a ballista bombardment to force the defenders back from the ramparts. The Britons' answer to the attackers as they came within range would have been from slingstones. These were discharged either from a leather strap-sling, or a staff-sling of wood and leather. One slingstone in the author's possession has a diameter of two inches and weighs seven ounces (200 grammes). It came from Maiden Castle near Dorchester, where the defenders had placed large stockpiles of suitable pebbles to employ at the gates, which with their associated earthworks were designed to provide a good field of defensive view. At close range, hand thrown stones could be effective up to a range of about 20 metres.

If necessary, the attackers could adopt a 'Testudo' ('Tortoise') armoured formation by linking their shields together over their heads against missiles. For the main assault, the Legion's foot soldiers were each equipped with two javelins; to be used before drawing the sword ('Gladius') and engaging in hand to hand combat. The Britons carried shields, used both throwing and thrusting spears and a sword which was usually fastened on the right side. Helmets were sometimes worn. Courage and passion were hallmarks of the Britons in battle. However, except when led by an outstanding commander such as Caratacus, able to impose order, the Britons were rarely able to match the disciplined might of the battle-hardened Roman legions.

In general, the Wessex hillforts yielded easily to the Second Legion's forces, and their inhabitants were transferred in the sixties after a final fruitless revolt.

Vespasian went on to subdue the southwest and establish a legionary base at Exeter. He was well rewarded by Claudius, pursuing a successful political career which reached its height in AD 69, when he succeeded Vitellius as the fourth man to be proclaimed emperor in that extraordinary year. A bluff personality, a good tactician and administrator, he was also a fair man and blessed with a sense of humour. He led the nation in ten years of good government and died in his bed – a rare occurrence with many emperors. He did have a close shave during Nero's tyrannical reign – when he fell asleep as the Emperor was entertaining the Court, singing at a party in Greece. Men had been murdered for less, but he was not only spared, but survived to repeat his transgression on another occasion, and to get away with it.

# Our Daily Bread

EVER SINCE MAN first harvested corn, there was a need to turn this into flour by milling. For many thousands of years this was done by hand. Use of a pestle and mortar evolved into the hand quern, in which a top millstone would be rotated against one below, with corn being poured into its centre, to be forced towards the circumference and then gathered into a container. This was a cheap method which could be carried on at home, with minimal risk of bureaucratic interference, but the process was extremely hard work – even with some refinements to make the turning easier.

The Roman miller Vitruvius has been credited with inventing power milling by water in about BC 25. Soon water mills operated by the Romans became common, and some began to be built in Britain shortly after Claudius' invasion in AD 43. When they departed in AD 410 knowledge of the technology lapsed and none appear

*A hand quern or grain grinding mill.*

to have been built again in this country for another 350 years or so. By the date of the Domesday Book survey in 1086, however, there were over 6,000 recorded mills in England but none in East Knoyle. Since they were taxable assets, it is safe to assume that there weren't any. By the early 1200s, the Bishop of Winchester had bought the Lordship of the Manor of Knoyle. Documents of his in the Hampshire Record

Office indicate that by that time he had a watermill built at Lushley in the west of the parish. However, locating it has been a problem as there are five separate fields with that name.

There is however a clue close to Moors Farm on the West Knoyle road, where a field with humps and bumps in it is called 'Mill Mead'. Without a geophysical survey there can be no certainty but there is evidence on the ground to suggest that a mill layout following the medieval pattern did exist there. The suggested millstream would have had a sluice on the line of the road to West Knoyle. Normally

*Mill Mead at Moors Farm, East Knoyle - probable site of the watermill at Lushley, East Knoyle.*

water would have been allowed to flow freely on in a semicircle, while water required for milling was made to run down a channel known as the 'the mill leat' or 'head water channel'. It then reached and passed through or over the mill wheel, which could have been any one of three types. An undershot wheel, a breastshot wheel or an overshot wheel – depending on how and where the flow of water reached the paddles. Power was transferred from the wheel along a horizontal axis, and then transferred by gearing through ninety degrees to turn a vertical shaft which caused the upper of the two horizontal millstones to rotate. The grain to be milled was fed downwards into the centre of these by a hopper, forced to the sides by the action of the stones and expelled as flour to be collected in a sack.

Once the water had passed the wheel it would run down the 'trail race' until rejoining the semicircular diverted stream flow. The mill building would have had some stone foundations but be mainly timber, wattle and daub with a thatched roof. Because the internal gears were made of wood, friction created heat which

*The probable mill leat at Moors Farm.*

could cause the flour dust to catch alight so that many mills were burnt down.

No record has come to light to show when it ceased to operate, but one may speculate that lowering of the water table since medieval times could have been responsible, or it may have been that the building of the East Knoyle windmill made wind power more economic. Two new sailyards were bought for this mill in 1377, and since the present structure which was brought into use in about 1536 rests on a circular plinth, this may tell us that here the cross trees were sunk into the earth to give stability to the original windmill – and to allow for a spar or a wheel arrangement to turn the sails into the wind. Windmills began to appear in Wessex in numbers in the 13th Century. Their gearing arrangements were very like those of the watermills, except that the driving shaft turned by the sails would have been angled upwards.

A watercolour painting by Jane Bouverie of Knoyle House dated 1873, shows the mill in action with two sails. The mill was still working in 1886, but soon afterwards began to decay, although it was still in reasonable order until 1911, with the structure topped by a gable cap and tailbox in the Somerset manner. The last recorded miller to come to light was Mr William Perry who was certainly actively milling in 1865, when he was listed as one of the village's principal citizens. He died in 1874, and was buried in St. Mary's churchyard. Estate workers cutting furze to repair a shelter on Mr Percy Wyndham's nine hole golf course in 1910 caused some damage, but disaster struck some six months later when the cap was used as a platform for village fireworks to mark King George V's Coronation. The machinery was removed during World War I but the tower survives as a domestic building with a splendid view over the Blackmore Vale.

Medieval lords of the manor put much effort into maintaining a tight grip on milling as a profitable source of income. All grain in the parish was supposed to be sent to the

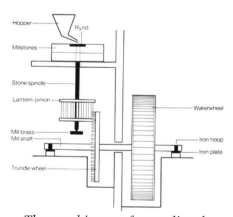

*The machinery of a medieval watermill (reproduced from The Mills of Medieval England, Holt, Richard 118, courtesy of Basil Blackwell Ltd).*

*The East Knoyle windmill in 1873, from a watercolour by Jane Bouverie of Knoyle House who recorded the parish scene for half a century from 1845.*

lord's mill for grinding, with a toll levied on each consignment – hand milling at home was severely discouraged. Where landlords directly managed their mills, wages for the miller were often meagre. The Winchester Pipe Roll for 1283 shows that the Bishop of Winchester (as Lord of the Manor of Knoyle) paid his millers an average of six shillings or less a year, with an allowance of a ton and a quarter of grain. Geoffrey Chaucer in writing his 'Canterbury Tales' singles out the miller as a despicable grasping character with very low morals, a suitable target for ridicule.

However, as recounted elsewhere, in Knoyle at least one family with milling connexions – the Goldsboroughs who originally came from Yorkshire – made the social transition into the ranks of the minor gentry.

There are a couple more milling riddles to solve. In the southeast of the parish runs 'Millbrook'; but despite the name there was no trace of any actual mill or any surviving memories of one until a few months ago. The brook was diverted in the early 1970's to serve the new parish sewage system. The original watercourse runs parallel to it but further to the east. Mr Cliff Sully has told the author that when doing some drainage work on a field on that alignment he came across a collection of carefully cut and shaped stonework with no obvious explanation. Maybe, just maybe, this is the missing mill.

In medieval times, there were three 'tithings' in the parish, of which Upton was one – a 'tithing' being an administrative unit originally consisting of ten households. It is therefore quite possible that Upton may have had its own mill. A possible line of the mill leat and sites of the millwheel can be deduced; but that is unfinished business.

*The possible site of a watermill at Upton.*

# The Admiral and his Lady
# Edward and Susan Pellew

T HIS IS THE STORY of a remarkable sailor, with a local connection. He was Edward Pellew, from a Cornish family whose father Samuel had been captain of a small Dover sailing packet. When his father died, the family returned to Penzance, mother remarried and Edward and his brothers John and Israel were brought up by relatives.

From an early age he had felt the sea in his blood; even while a twelve year-old at Truro Grammar School where he was regarded by his headmaster as a difficult and strong willed boy. This was unlikely to have worried Edward, as his mind was firmly set on a commissioned career in the Royal Navy. Two factors were to work in his favour; the first being that the Royal Navy was racing to expand in the face of a threat from Spain to annex the Falkland Islands. For Pellew, the most practical way to reach the bottom rung of his chosen career was to be accepted as a 'Captain's Servant'. The regulations clearly laid down that to reach the rank of Lieutenant (the lowest commissioned level in the Navy) all new entrants had to serve at least six years at sea including two as a Midshipman. Lord Falmouth, brother of the famous admiral Boscawen, was the man to make this possible.

The Pellew family had at one time been substantial landowners around Falmouth and in Britain's American colonies. While most of this land had been lost Lord Falmouth still recognised an obligation to help the Pellews when he could. Admiral Boscawen had advanced one Captain John Stott from being just a competent boatswain to becoming a well regarded commander of a man-of-war. Stott, who had earned his promotions on merit, was nevertheless conscious that he owed the Admiral, and by extension Lord Falmouth, an obligation.

Admiral Boscawen, through his brother 'invited' Stott to take young Edward on strength, and there was nothing unusual about this, except that it was an invitation bound to be accepted. So, on Boxing Day 1770 at the age of thirteen and a half, a tall robust-looking but somewhat nervous boy climbed up the side of His Majesty's Ship 'Juno' lying at Portsmouth and reported for duty. A 'Captain's servant' was in reality what might be described as a probationary midshipman. Juno was a fifth rate frigate commanded by Capt Stott, which set off for the Falkland Islands with orders to re-establish Britain as their rightful owner – a task to be undertaken once more in two hundred years' time.

On his arrival, the threat melted away, and there was no loss of life. After this successful outcome, in 1772 the ship's complement transferred to Juno's sister ship HMS Alarm for duties in the Mediterranean where Pellew earned promotion to Midshipman. Edward was a quick learner, Midshipman Pellew being further advanced to Master's Mate. Three years later Edward and another 'Middy' nearly brought their careers to an abrupt end. They had drawn a saucy cartoon of the Captain's mistress, who was on board at the time. A furious Captain Stott found out, put the two pranksters ashore at Marseilles with no money and sailed off.

Pellew's luck was in, for in port was a merchant ship whose captain had been friendly with his father, so he was able to reach England via Lisbon. Once home, he sought out Admiral Boscawen and successfully pleaded with him to remain in the Royal Navy. He was sent as an Able Seaman to the frigate Blonde, commanded by Captain Pownall. There he soon buckled down to work and began to show his outstanding qualities of seamanship, courage and leadership. The Blonde was conveying General 'Gentleman Johnny' Burgoyne in charge of the reinforcements being sent in 1776 to cope with the growing conflict with the rebellious American colonists. When the Blonde reached Quebec, the crew under Pellew were detached for 'Lake Service'. The task entailed constructing a small flotilla of fighting ships on the shore of Lake Champlain to destroy the rebel warships operating on the lake and so open the way to New York. Pellew, restored to Midshipman rank and Mr Midshipman Brown were then detached to serve on the newly constructed armed schooner HMS Carleton commanded by Lieutenant Dacres . She found herself under relentless attack, putting up a fierce fight during the Battle of Valcour Island, but losing half her crew killed or wounded. With Dacres unconscious, and his deputy also out of action, Pellew found himself in command. The courage and skill of this 19 year-old in extricating the Carleton from a most dangerous situation did not go unnoticed. In the following year, still as a Midshipman, he was the sole naval officer on General Burgoyne's disastrous expedition which ended with surrender at Saratoga. The Commander had not forgotten Pellew, and though far junior to everyone else present, he was summoned to attend the council of war. When the end came, the General chose Pellew to carry back the despatches to London announcing the fateful news of the surrender at Saratoga. There was a bittersweet element for him personally. He carried a recommendation for promotion to Lieutenant, which was put into effect. However he also brought to his family news of the death of his younger brother. John Pellew had been serving as an ensign in The British army, and died defending a fortification at Saratoga.

*Butterstakes Farm in 2000, rebuilt in Victorian times using some of the original stonework. The building was demolished in 2002.*

Six years later two important events happened: Pellew was promoted Post Captain at the early age of 26, and he got married. His choice fell on Susan Frowd, whose family had been merchants in Salisbury for generations, and whose father was James Frowd, living with his wife and family at Butterstakes Farm, Sedgehill near Shaftesbury. According to him he met her 'accidentally when passing though a retired village before she had ever heard a gun or seen the sea'. Susan was, however, no country bumpkin but a much admired young lady later described as 'vivacious, fascinating and pleasing

*The present Butterstakes Farm in 2007.*

to all wherever she and her husband set up residence'. She was also a lady of decided character, deeply religious, devoted to her husband and astute at managing the family finances. The marriage took place not in St Catherine's Sedgehill but at the larger church of St. Mary's East Knoyle on May the 28th 1783.

With the USA established as an independent nation, the Treasury – not for the last time – laid up the greater part of the Navy and placed many of its officers on the unemployed list receiving only half pay. Pellew was among the victims languishing ashore – and except for a spell in command of HMS Winchester and then HMS Salisbury – was reduced to farming on a family property at Treverry in Cornwall – for which as a man of action he was temperamentally unsuited and at which he was not apparently much good! Susan was happy to have him at home with their growing family, but he was frustrated – even though he appreciated her affection and financial skills. He fretted at being unable to continue to develop his promising naval career – and this made him difficult to live with at times.

War with France broke out in February 1793, and after reminding his patron Lord Falmouth of his availability, Pellew was given command of a 40 gun frigate, the Nymphe. She was a fine little ship but with no rigging, spars or crew. In the way of the Royal Navy when seeking reinforcements, the men of a small merchant vessel were pressganged for a start. Then 80 unemployed Cornish tin miners voluntarily offered their services . . . none of whom had ever been to sea. A mate of the small merchant vessel Venus had agreed to transfer to the King's service, so that on setting sail he had 36 Royal Marines, a hundred landsmen and six seamen capable of taking the wheel on a ship designed for a complement of two hundred and twenty.

Enlisting the tin miners was not quite so strange a recruitment as one might think. Although landsmen, the miners were used to the self-discipline and coordination essential in a dangerous occupation. Pellew immediately set in hand a rigorous training programme, but was not afraid to lead by example. On one occasion when he had ordered the watch aloft to take in a reef in very difficult weather conditions, the men were startled to hear a well known voice from the extreme end of one of the crosstrees urging them on. It was their captain.

Three months later he met the French frigate Cleopatre off Start Point and after both captains courteously raised their hats to each other, battle commenced. The French ship was well commanded with an experienced crew. After an hour's gun duel in which Pellew's hard training of his men paid off handsomely, the French were forced to surrender, and the Cleopatre was brought into Portsmouth as a prize with her flag below the union jack. Pellew's opposing Captain was killed in the encounter, his last action being to try to swallow his commission, which he had mistaken for the French code of secret signals. The attempt failed, the code fell intact into Pellew's hands and was duly forwarded to the Admiralty – not quite as significant as the capture of an enigma machine nearly a century and a half later, but very welcome nevertheless. The victorious commander was generous in his praise of his opponent Capitaine Mullon and in providing practical help to his widow. The nation rejoiced, King George III announced the capture while watching the opera at Covent Garden and Edward Pellew was awarded a knighthood. For the next year Nymphe was tasked with operating independently in the Channel – just the kind of commission that Sir Edward relished. Then Pellew and his crew were transferred to the Arethusa (the 'saucy Arethusa' of the sea song) and later to HMS Indefatigable. While on Indefatigable, Pellew attended a concert in Lisbon . He was impressed by the talent of a young black musician playing second violin, and

*Joseph Emidy, violinist in an ensemble at a concert in Truro after 1799; possibly at the Assembly Room, or at a private residence (reproduced by courtesy of the Royal Cornwall Museum).*

promptly pressganged him aboard to replace a missing ship's fiddler. This ex-slave, captured as a boy in West Africa, was taken to Brazil by his master, who soon discovered the lad's love of music and paid for him to receive lessons. Moving to Portugal with his master, just four years later, Joseph Antonio Emidy gained a place in the Lisbon Opera Orchestra. He received his discharge from the Royal Navy at Falmouth in 1799. He then built a substantial career for himself as composer, teacher, performer and artist throughout Cornwall. None of his original works have survived, although the music historian, composer and instrumentalist Jon Rose on his website has described how he has composed a concerto for violin and chamber orchestra, making use of the elements which are likely to have formed Emidy's musical character. Joseph died in 1835 at the age of 60 and is buried in Kenwyn churchyard, Truro.

*Joseph Emidy's tombstone in Kenwyn churchyard (reproduced courtesy of Wikipedia, the free encyclopedia http:// wikipedia.org/wiki/ Joseph_Antonio_Emidy).*

On January the 26th 1796, Pellew again came to honourable notice. Indefatigable had docked at Plymouth and Edward in full uniform with sword was travelling with Susan to have dinner with the Vicar of the Exmoor parish of Charles. This was the Reverend Dr Hawker, a retired surgeon, who had become acquainted with Pellew when serving in Plymouth as surgeon to the Royal Marines. They had become good friends and were to remain so for the rest of their lives. In Pellew's words: ' Susan and I were driving to a dinner party in Plymouth when we saw crowds running to the Hoe and hearing it was a wreck I left the carriage to take her on and joined the crowd'. Another account says that 'he sprang out of the carriage and ran off with the rest' – as Susan watched with dismay.

The wrecked ship was the Troop Transport 'Dutton' on her way to the West Indies, with part of the 2nd (Queen's) Regiment embarked. The voyage had already taken seven weeks. There were over four hundred soldiers on board, many of them sick with fever, about a hundred seamen and women and children too. Driven into Plymouth Sound by the wild winter weather, and the gale increasing in the afternoon, Dutton's master sought a position of greater safety. Although the pilots on board did not realise it at first, a buoy off Mount Batten broke adrift, the ship touched on a shoal and the rudder was carried away. Now unmanageable, Dutton grounded under the Royal Citadel, rolling heavily. At the second roll she became partially dismasted.

As Pellew arrived at the beach, in a disgraceful display of cowardice, the last of the officers reached the shore from the ship. As Pellew was to write to a friend much later 'I saw the loss of the whole five or six hundred was inevitable without somebody to direct them'. Having urged the officers to return, which they refused to do, he then vainly offered rewards to pilots and others belonging to the port to board the wreck; but all of them thought this to be too hazardous to

*The troopship 'Dutton', wrecked under the Royal Citadel, Plymouth on 26 January 1796.*

attempt. In exasperation, with Susan looking on from a distance, he cried out 'Then I will go myself'.

There was still one rope in position, the one on which the officers and a few others had come ashore, and so with his sword still buckled on he had himself hauled through the surf. As he reached the ship, the mainmast which had already toppled towards the shore, crashed on to his back. At the time he ignored the pain and set about restoring order. He announced himself, assumed command, and with just the bosun to help him re-established order. He assured the people that everyone would be saved if they quietly obeyed his orders, that he himself would be the last to leave the wreck, but that he would run anyone through who disobeyed him. He was not in fact forced to take this drastic step, although he did have to lay about him with the flat of his sword to subdue a rabble of drunken men – for some of the soldiers had broken into the liquor store and were now drunk. One account states that his announcement 'was received with three hearty cheers, which was echoed by the multitude on shore'. No doubt the relief at finding someone taking positive action was very great, but one suspects that the cheers may have been a bit ragged! With some help from his own ship Indefatigable (whose officers did not at first know that their Captain was aboard the wreck), the efforts of a slowly organised shore party and some small boats which eventually managed to come alongside, everyone was safely rescued. Pellew was not actually the last to leave, as the gallant bosun refused to go before him.

He was soon reunited with his wife, who nursed him for a week as he recovered from the effects of his back injury and exposure. While convalescing, he expressed his satisfaction at being able to bring the women, the children and the sick safely ashore. Nothing, he said, had impressed him more strongly than when seeking to rescue a baby just three weeks old; he had watched the struggle of the mother's feelings before she would entrust the infant to his care. Equally, nothing afforded him more pleasure than the success of his attempt to save it.

A well-earned baronetcy was his reward. Sir Edward, Baronet, was now able to combine living with his wife and six children at an elegant rented house in Falmouth with command of what was probably the best squadron in the fleet. Two of the sons had naval careers, and one became a bishop.

A skilful action against the massive French man of war the 74 gun 'Droits de l'Homme', brought him further fame – and prize money for his crew. However, in the next year he was despatched against his will to take command of 'Impetueux' a sound ex-French ship of the line but with a crew known to be on the verge of mutiny. Two months later they refused to obey orders, but they picked the wrong man to confront. He quickly restored discipline, three mutineers were sentenced to hang and a further five were flogged round the fleet. Impetueux was never a happy ship and he was glad when his tour of duty ended in April 1802, as peace with France was achieved for a while.

Peacetime living, with his family at home, was wearisome to him and proved a strain on his relationship with Susan. In a letter to his friend Alex Broughton he said she was, 'obstinately bent on resistance to my wishes, and I assure you she has made me miserable, it is a great and lamentable misfortune that she will not repose more confidence in me . . . all would be well if she would cease resistance. It is terrible with two nice girls at home to hear domestic contention, and therefore my dear Alex I am going abroad, I hope with a good Command – time may soften her feelings, she is a good creature and the best of Wives, but she does not see far enough into these things and has painted a fancied path of life in domestic retirement with me at her elbow – it is all affection in the end'

After urging from Lord St. Vincent (1st Lord of the Admiralty) he put his name forward and was successfully elected one of two MPs for Barnstaple at the General Election in July 1802. Lady Pellew had a strong dislike for London and was unenthusiastic about his desire to enter Parliament. He found parliamentary manoeuvring distasteful, and spent much time and energy badgering the Admiralty to give him another seagoing command. He even addressed a letter to Admiral Lord Nelson, in which he made a strong plea to be allowed to serve under the Admiral's command. In his reply, dated May the 1st 1804, Nelson showed a keen appreciation of Sir Edward's qualities and hinted that he could be a possible successor. He wrote: 'I am truly sensible of the honour you do me in expressing a wish to serve under me, but you have always my dear Sir Edward proved yourself so equal to command a fleet that it would be a sin to place you in any other situation.'. He went on to foresee an impending retirement: 'My services are nearly at an end for in addition to other infirmities I am nearly blind – however I hope to fight one more Battle and then unless my health and sight mends, which is not very likely, I expect perhaps to lay down the cudgels and console myself with the Idea that there are so many more able officers than ever I would pretend to be to take them up'. He signed off as: 'Your much obliged friend and servant'.

Sir Edward made just one speech in the House of Commons. This was in 1804, when he was incensed by what he saw as unfair criticism of the Lord St. Vincent as 1st Lord of the Admiralty. He clearly and cogently refuted this, point by point, much in the manner

*Rear Admiral Edward Pellew, 1st Viscount Exmouth: Detail from the painting by Lawrence (reproduced by kind permission of his descendant, Lieutenant Colonel F.H. (Hugo) Pellew).*

of Winston Churchill in the darkest days of World War II. He sat down to thunderous applause, was soon promoted Rear Admiral and became C in C East Indies.

His arrival in Madras to take command in 1805 was the start of a very successful period for Pellew, both professionally and financially. There was a numerically strong hostile Dutch fleet in the area at Batavia Roads, but it was not in good fettle and no match for the Royal Navy. Many prizes were taken, with prize money distributed to all ranks, a welcome addition to their meagre wages. Pellew's portion was probably in excess of £100,000 (worth millions at today's values).

The author Thomas Bayly, writing a few years later said that 'Absence makes the heart grow fonder'. In Pellew's case this certainly seems to be true, as another letter from Madras to his friend Alex Broughton in July 1807 makes clear: 'I have won a lottery ticket worth £26,000' (actually the prize money from the 'San Raffael') and a draft to that amount goes to my dearly beloved Susan – to reward her for all her tender love for me and for her anxious endeavors (sic) to rear her family in the paths of Innocence and Virtue, to become one day an honour to their Country . . . Would you have believed that your Ugly, Uninteresting and Uneducated cub, your old friend Ned Pellew, would ever have become an Admiral, a Commander-in-Chief, a Colonel of Marines, a Baronet, and a man with a purse weighing fifty thousand pounds?' He also comments that Susan should do more

*Westcliffe (now 'Bitton') House at Teignmouth, overlooking the estuary.*

*gadding* in Bath to get her Girl married, and that young Men must now be sought for. Pellew suggested to Broughton that his friend should join his wife Susan and her daughter Julia in that elegant city for six weeks. In a final confidence, he ends the letter with: 'She (Susan) has turned out well and I would not part with her for the Princess Charlotte, (but) don't tell her so or I shall never be able to manage her'.

By 1809, the East Indies climate was taking its toll as he ended his tour of duty without a relief in post. 'I am full of East India bile', he wrote 'running to belly and grey as a badger'.

With Edward and his wife now financially secure, Susan arranged for them to settle at a country estate at Canonteign near Christow; but her husband disagreed, preferring Westcliffe House, an elegant 18th Century property in a fine position overlooking the estuary at Teignmouth. It was later renamed Bitton House and is well maintained in its present role of Local Council offices. Canonteign was however a family home for their descendants, until being sold ten years or so ago.

Like out of work actors, Pellew 'rested' for a while before being appointed C-in-C Mediterranean in 1811. It was a busy time, in which the fleet again seized numerous enemy ships. During the 'Hundred Days' campaign in France leading up to Napoleon's final defeat at Waterloo, Toulon had risen in support of the Bourbon king, and Pellew was to be found (almost in comic opera fashion) at the head of a force riding towards the action . . .

His final deed on active service came in 1816, after Napoleon had been finally disposed of. He was ordered to compel the Dey of Algiers, who was the last active slave trading ruler in the Mediterranean, to submit and to release over a thousand slave captives. Nelson had once said that the Algiers fortress could not be taken with less than 25 ships – Pellew had initially proposed using just five ships of the line! In the event there were 17 Royal Naval vessels augmented by a Dutch

*The Battle of Algiers 1816, by Chambers. Pellew's flagship the Queen Charlotte is in the centre background, with the dark flag at the mainmast.*

The DEY of ALGIERS, Surrendering to LORD EXMOUTH 1085 Christian Slaves and all the MONEY Received for Ransom, amounting to 382 500 DOLLARS Aug 28 1816.

*A popular contemporary print, purporting to show the Dey of Algiers surrendering to Admiral Pellew after the Battle of Algiers, with some of the released slaves.*

squadron of 6 ships, which made a valuable contribution. The enemy force included 40,000 troops, 4 frigates, five large corvettes and a fortress bristling like a porcupine with cannon. After a bruising all day engagement against the enemy's fleet and shore batteries, the enemy arsenal was set on fire, the sea defences were shattered and the enemy fleet effectively destroyed. Shortly afterwards the Dey apologised, released over three thousand slaves, including a few Britons, and agreed to renew the treaty which he had so unwisely broken. Pellew took the Dey's submission, somewhat inaccurately recorded in a cartoon reproduced in inns and public places across the land. The Dey's remaining time in power was short. Some of his subjects blamed him for a series of misfortunes, and he was murdered by strangulation in the following year.

After the battle, Pellew was 'advanced to the dignity of a viscount' and his coat of arms augmented. The name 'Algiers' was added as a second motto. Honours were showered upon him. The Kings of Holland, Spain and Sardinia conferred on him orders of Knighthood, while the Pope sent him a valuable cameo. The City of London made him a freeman, and a diamond-decorated sword was presented to him at a Lord Mayor's banquet. His own squadron officers subscribed to present him with a costly silver model of part of the Algiers fortress. Pellew acquired another sort of immortality with several sets of islands named after him. The Sir Edward Pellew group of islands lie in the Gulf of Carpentaria near the mouth of the McArthur River. They were named by Matthew Flinders who visited them in 1802. Composed of barren sandstone, they are now promoted as a fishing area teeming with barramundi, snapper, coral trout, mackerel, marlin and other fish. There is also Pellew Island off Jamaica, sitting off the end of a coral reef, a superb natural setting with fine snorkelling and swimming. It is currently threatened with a development of villas, which environmentalists are seeking to prevent.

Finally, there is the Republic of Belau (formerly the Pellew Islands), 500 miles east of the Philippines – described as an unspoiled marine paradise in travel literature.

Viscount Exmouth (as he now became) lived the rest of his life in Devon, receiving a final promotion to Vice Admiral in the year before his death on January the 23rd 1833 at home in Westcliffe House.

Nelson has Trafalgar Square, with his column, Landseer's lions and a secure place in the nation's affections. Although justly honoured in his lifetime, in England Pellew is publicly remembered now by just 'The Exmouth Arms' in Euston, an interesting display in Teignmouth Museum and memorials in St. James's Parish Church, Christow, nearby.

Although a stern, even fierce disciplinarian, Pellew was careful of his men's lives and welfare. He led from the front and never asked a man to do anything of which he himself was not capable. On more than one occasion he dived off his ship to rescue seamen who had fallen overboard or to evaluate damage done to the hull. He was prone to pushing the career interests of his family, sometimes beyond their abilities – nepotism which while reckoned unacceptable today was pretty commonplace in his own time. It is said that he was reluctant to delegate authority to others – and when he was forced to do so, they sometimes let him down. Personally modest, he made a point of bringing the good performance of subordinates to the notice of higher authority. His talents were, perhaps, most apparent during his time as a frigate captain, outstanding amongst the many very good captains who were his contemporaries. It was certainly a time when he was professionally most happy. Throughout his 63 years of

*The Exmouth Arms in Euston, London.*

service in the Royal Navy he served both it and the country with gallantry and distinction.

Perhaps Admiral Codrington, victor at the Battle of Navarino against the Turks, had a point when he said that men worked well for Nelson for fear of not pleasing him, while working for Pellew for fear of displeasing him, a subtle but vital distinction.

During the Battle for Algiers, Pellew flew a large dark green flag with white cotton circles of varying sizes appliquéd to one side from the mainmast of his flagship, the Queen Charlotte. There have been many repairs of navy blue wool rectangles and darnings in navy, light blue and light brown wool. It is thought to have been perhaps a Barbary standard. For many years it hung over his tomb. It was used on occasion as a pall, and even flew from a flagstaff in Christow churchyard. Then it apparently disappeared. Now back in the possession of the present Lord Exmouth and his family, but on long loan to Teignmouth and Shaldon Museum; it is in very frail condition. An active campaign is seeking to raise the necessary funds for its restoration.

Susan's memorial in Christow church speaks of 'Susan, Viscountess Exmouth, daughter of James Frowd Esq. of Sedgehill, near Shaftesbury, Wiltshire' as: 'A pious, faithful and beloved wife, and exemplary mother, and friend. Respected and esteemed by all who knew her sterling worth'. Such testimonials sometimes exaggerate, but this one seems to have got it just about right.

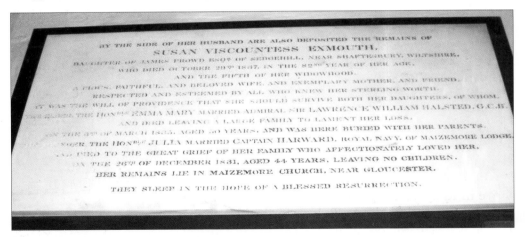

*Susan, Lady Exmouth's memorial in Christow church.*

# Knoylians for Ninety Years

WHEREAS Admiral Pellew's direct involvement with Knoyle, though significant was brief, George King's has to date spanned nine decades.

George's grandfather, also George, was a stonemason for the Seymour Estate at Knoyle House. His father Bert was born in Cowley near Oxford, coming to Knoyle in 1911 with responsibility for the string of horses belonging to his employer Lord 'Teddy' Mostyn who had rented Knoyle House for the hunting season.

Shortly afterwards, in mid September, he joined the crowds at Knoyle Feast, originally held to commemorate the Church of St. Mary's patronal festival. Amid the village band, blowing away, the swings, the stalls and the general activity, he met Abigail and they fell in love.

Abigail lived in a pretty tenanted thatched stone cottage in Wise Lane, the road that runs from the Square up to The Green, sadly demolished during World War II.

At the end of the 1911-12 hunting season with the South and West Wilts Hunt, Bert had left the village, but Abigail, now his fiancée, stayed behind. When the First World War broke out in August 1914, Lord Mostyn took Bert and his horses into the Army – a fairly common happening among the aristocracy in those days – and they soon found themselves at the front in France.

The engaged couple planned that when Bert could get some home leave, they would get married, but in the event the path of true love did not run smoothly. In 1916, Bert was given ten days leave; but the day before he was due to arrive in Knoyle a telegram was delivered to 8 Wise Lane ordering him to 'Return forthwith'! This galvanised Abigail into action. The East Knoyle Rector was not helpful, so Abigail walked the two miles to Hindon and enlisted the aid of the Vicar, who obtained a special marriage licence. So, Bert arrived in Knoyle on Saturday, they were married in Hindon Church on Sunday and he returned to France on Monday.

*George King, aged 2, with his mother Abigail (centre) at 8 Wise Lane, the family home.*

Bert returned safely at the end of 1918 from his service with the Royal Welch Fusiliers, and George was born in September 1919. Bert became a dairyman, working for a local farmer, at Red House Farm at the South end of the village in the area known as The Turnpike.

In the 21st Century, the highway authorities tend to keep a sharp eye open for trees that might become dangerous and fall across the road. Eighty years ago in the nineteen twenties, when traffic was less dense, things were rather different. A law had in fact just been passed requiring owners of elm trees at the side of roads to have them trimmed or cut down, but the process was expected to be spread over a number of years.

The greatest danger was naturally foreseen as occurring during storms and high winds; but it was on a calm summer's day that disaster struck at the roadside between Park Farm and Gaston field, later used by the village football team and now bisected by the bypass. Four people were bowling along happily in an open tourer car travelling north with two ladies sitting in the back. There was then a row of elm trees at the edge of the field. As the car passed by, a large branch broke off the main trunk and fell across the back seat, striking the two lady passengers. Bert and his family were eating their midday dinner when there was a cry at the gate 'Bert, Bert, help wanted, come and bring your cross cut' (saw). Within minutes over half a dozen people were at the scene. George remembers seeing his father using the cross cut to sever the branch. Bert then helped to lift the ladies free and lay them out in the field. They must have been killed almost instantly, but the two front passengers were rescued only suffering from shock.

Within the next two years, all the roadside elms were cut down and removed by a contractor ten miles away to Warminster. Each day the timber wagons loaded with four or five trunks would set off at 4 p.m. on the ten mile journey, pulled by four shire horses.

*The Battle cruiser HMS Repulse in 1937.*

*HMS Indomitable, part of Task Force 67, in 1945.*

Bert later worked as a groom and handyman for Mrs Ruperta Shand at Slades, an attractive property below the former Wyndham family mansion at Clouds.

George's childhood was a very happy one, shattered at the age of eleven by the death of his mother at the age of 41, after a short illness. In due course his father married again, this time the household's cook, Annie Fraser, a Scots lady whose culinary skills are still remembered in the village. Bert's affection for Annie blossomed when Mrs Shand allowed her cook to make a special meal for Bert when he was ill – a kind deed about which she was somewhat rueful when Annie in due course left her employment. She was a good stepmother, but George became restless, and at age 15 he applied to join the Navy.

After a year in training, he joined the battle cruiser HMS Repulse at Portsmouth for a two and a half year commission in the Mediterranean. Routine was broken when George and Repulse returned to England to take part in the famous Naval Review at Spithead to mark the Coronation on May the 12th 1937 of King George VI and his Queen, Elizabeth later to be known and loved as the 'Queen Mum' after the King's premature death in 1952. This was the occasion when the BBC commentator, Retired Commander Tommy Woodroffe was overenthusiastic in describing the floodlighting of the Fleet: 'The Fleet's lit up, the whole . . . fleet's lit up'.

George spent the second World War in five different aircraft carriers, notably HMS Indomitable, flagship of the British Pacific Fleet, commanded by Captain (later Admiral Sir John) Eccles RN. In 1945 as part of Task Force 67, she was on

*One of HMS Indomitable's Hellcat aircraft taking off. George King was in charge of servicing them.*

her way to help the Americans invade Okinawa, when a mutiny broke out. Petty Officer King, in charge of servicing the ship's 12 Hellcat aircraft, was in a position to observe the action.

The fleet was anchored off a desolate coral atoll on the equator. The ship's company had been cooped up for more than a year, the food ration was inadequate, and the seamen were fed up. One day, on being piped to dinner, the men instead clipped down the hatches, remained below, refusing to allow the mess trays down, and roundly booed George and the mess cooks as they attempted to serve the meal. As the Commander (the ship's Second in Command) strode across the deck as if to go below through the turret that George had just passed he got an even bigger 'Boo' . . . The said Commander shot back on to the Flight Deck 'like a champagne cork' strode past George and the cooks and disappeared below.

We know what happened to Capt Pellew's mutineers, but Capt Eccles handled it differently. About ten minutes after the Commander's encounter with the mutineers, the Captain called the hands to muster on the Flight deck: 'I understand there has been a bit of trouble up forward over the food' he said. 'I want every mess deck to appoint a representative to meet me forward of the windbreak in 15 minutes' time'. The mutiny was over, The CinC Pacific authorised a ration increase, and the ship got on with its duties, although the Second in Command and 1st Lieutenant were posted out.

*A Japanese Zeke plane, with its suicidal Kamikaze pilot diving on HMS Indomitable. Note the bubbling wake as the ship takes a sharp turn to starboard in an effort to avoid being hit.*

*HMS Indomitable's sister ship HMS Formidable suffered damage and casualties from a Kamikaze attack.*

A different excitement came a bit later when a Japanese 'Zeke' aircraft with its Kamikaze pilot crept under the radar beam, came in from 300 feet and dived at an angle of 45 degrees, to hit the deck to port by the bridge. Because the ship had turned hard astarboard the plane skidded along the flight deck and went over the port side, blowing up when it hit the water, causing no casualties. All four carriers (Indomitable, Indefatigable, Illustrious and Formidable) were hit but Formidable fared the worst with significant damage and loss of life.

*HMS Indomitable lying in Hong Kong in August 1945. Note the low skyline at that time!*

With the atomic bombs on Hiroshima and Nagasaki instrumental in bringing about a Japanese surrender, Indomitable entered Hong Kong in August 1945 to reassert the British sovereignty which was to last for another 50 years or so.

George and Indomitable returned home to be greeted by his wife and two sons at Portsmouth on December the 20th, though like the rest of the ship's complement he had lost weight, in his case two stones – leading one wag to quip that the ship had returned 'with a skeleton crew'.

Six years later Lieutenant

*Captain Eccles watches as the Japanese General signs the surrender document with his brush in Hong Kong, while an Admiral awaits his turn.*

King was back in the Far East on HMS Whitesand Bay for the Korean War . After subsequently commanding the Minesweeper HMS Sheraton, he retired as a Lieutenant Commander in 1964. When his wife died ten years later, he in due course married Joan and they live in contented retirement at Warsash near Southampton.

At 87, he still keeps up with village affairs and visits on special occasions, the most recent being the re-opening of the Post Office and Shop.

*(right) Lieutenant Commander George King RN, who had a tour of duty commanding the Mine-sweeper HMS Sheraton. (far right) George and Joan King at their home in Warsash, Hampshire in 2007.*

# A Tale of Two Services
# Francis Swain

ANOTHER NAVAL MAN with Knoyle connexions is the subject of this chapter. Like Edward Pellew, he served on HMS Indefatigable (though in a 24,000 ton version over two centuries later); and like George King he was part of Task Force 67 in the Pacific in World War II. Details of his remarkable career did not become generally known until after his death in 2007.

It was late 1944. Fleet Air Arm pilot Francis Swain was embarked on Indefatigable, tasked by the American Admiral Nimitz to destroy the Japanese oil refineries on the island of Sumatra, which were supplying three quarters of Japanese requirements of aviation fuel. Sixty aircraft took part in the first attack, with 887 Fleet Air Arm Squadron's Seafires flying in close formation at 50 feet in thick cloud and heavy rain from an altitude of 500 feet upwards.

'Close formation' meant keeping the Seafire's propeller twelve feet behind and just below the aircraft in front, with no radio contact permitted. An unknown plane cut across him just 30 feet away and disappeared into the murk; then a few seconds later Francis emerged from thick cloud and flying on instruments into bright sunshine, with aircraft speeding in all directions.

'Needless to say' Francis wrote afterwards, 'the Japs saw us too'. Heavy, but fortunately inaccurate anti-aircraft fire made life difficult and dogfights erupted. Francis diverted his course to rescue an American Corsair fighter that was under attack and saw off three Japanese Zero fighters – by which time the bombers were on their way back to the aircraft carriers. He emptied his ammunition into a couple of oil storage tanks and set off for home. The Seafire variant of the famous Spitfire could only operate at fairly short range, and despite being fitted with extra fuel tanks, his plane was now low on fuel. Francis was sweating profusely from the humidity and the heat, including apparently in his left boot, and his left leg was sticky too. He felt very tired.

Francis' own account, written for his family later, explained what happened next: 'There were only two aircraft ahead of me as I approached the 'Indefatigable'. I lined up to land . . . things seemed all very grey and misty; very odd, there couldn't be any mist in the cockpit! Busy now, flaps, wheels down . . . jammed, open throttle, waggle wings . . . over fly and go round again. Better try and release the undercarriage first. Fuel gauge nil – running on vapour! Noticed many more aircraft coming, which must be low on fuel too . . . cannot crash land on the deck in case I blocked it and other aircraft might have to ditch in the sea. Up through those clouds again to 10,000 feet. Clear now, so dive and try to flick the undercarriage free. 1500 feet, pull stick back hard. Blacked out and had to guess level flight and direction away from incoming aircraft . . . left boot very squelchy.
Can now see through my mist, one more try before I ditch near a destroyer and hope to be picked up. Nose down again . . . open throttle . . . stick back . . . blind . . . guess level flight – light comes on. Where's the carrier? . . . look round.. find it . . . cannot think straight . . . here we go.. caught the arrester wire . . . starboard plane leg collapsed . . . thump!!'

That was the end of the sortie, as Francis discovered when he awoke in the sick bay several hours later. All the aircraft had been recovered whilst he was standing off and trying to get the undercarriage down. Although it collapsed on impact with the deck, there had been no fire – there had been no fuel left to catch alight. There was anti aircraft damage and some shrapnel stuck in the landing gear machinery. The fuel line had been punctured, and the pilot too – hence the boot full of blood (not 'sweat') and Francis' misty vision.

*HMS Indefatigable, from which Francis Swain flew his Seafire aircraft to attack oil refineries on Sumatra.*

Fourteen aircraft had landed safely while Francis stood his aircraft off. If he had clogged up the deck, up to 40% of the planes might have been lost. For his outstandingly skilful and courageous action, Francis was awarded the Distinguished Service Order.

In 1945 Indefatigable was in Sydney for a while and then took part in air strikes on Formosa. She was the first British ship to be hit by Japanese suicidal 'kamikaze' attacks but was fully operational again within the hour. Indefatigable flew a third of all Fleet Air Arm sorties in two busy months between March and May 1945, and flew the last sortie of the war on August the 15th, when the Seafires of Francis' squadron shot down eight Japanese aircraft.

Francis then left the Navy, but saw action again in the Korean War; this time as an Army Officer in the Royal Engineers. By April 1951, the Chinese had entered the war on the North Korean side and 29 Commonwealth Brigade was deployed on the line of the River Imjin defending over seven miles of river frontage against a seemingly unstoppable Chinese advance. This was the epic struggle in which the Gloucesters, the

*Francis Swain's two cap badges: Royal Navy then Royal Engineers.*

Royal Northumberland Fusiliers and their supporting artillery were to earn lasting fame for their resistance against overwhelming odds.

However, at this point in early April, the infantry defensive positions were poorly prepared without deep slit trenches, mines or barbed wire. In the view of the Engineer Squadron commander 'No special precautions had been taken'. Francis was ordered to take eight three ton lorries loaded with engineering stores and a troop of Sappers to set up defensive works designed to slow the Chinese advance. As the convoy arrived in a forward area, it was clear that the position was under severe attack from the side of the hill, which was covered with 'ants' – Chinese troops en masse, some only a hundred yards away. He sent word to his Troop Sergeant with the convoy to come up and help, took over a Bren light machine gun from a wounded soldier, and with one of his men refilling the magazines as they emptied, remembered standing up on the ridge and firing repeatedly downhill into the 'ants'. With the aid of the Royal Engineer Sergeant and his men, the defenders then rallied some of the wounded infantry and stemmed the tide as the Chinese and North Koreans gave up and ran back down the hill. Only four of Francis' men were slightly wounded and he later scolded them for being so foolish as to stand on the ramparts in full view of the enemy while firing their weapons. They replied 'The enemy didn't manage to touch you Sir, did they? – so what did we have to worry about!'

As soon as they could, the Royal Ulster Rifles, held in reserve, came forward to relieve the Fusiliers and Francis' Troop of Sappers, who were able to withdraw. As has been well recorded, the courage of the Commonwealth Brigade succeeded in halting the Chinese advance and inflicted huge casualties. In this action Francis and his Royal Engineers played a gallant and significant part – and for his leadership by example this modest unassuming man was awarded the Military Cross. This is a decoration for gallantry that is always hard earned – it doesn't come up with the rations! I have not found any record of it ever being held in combination with a DSO gained in naval service.

# HMT Kingston Agate

T HE LAST NAVAL ITEM is a community connexion, between the two villages of East Knoyle and its neighbour Sedgehill with HMS Kingston Agate which they each adopted during Warship Week in March 1942 and were presented with certificates by the Lords Commissioners of the Admiralty to mark the event.

55 years later, when I first sought to find out more, no one seemed to know any further details. However, with the help of the Public Records Office at Kew, the Imperial War Museum, a number of published accounts and the invaluable help of a number of personal contacts – a remarkable story emerged.

Kingston Agate was a 464 ton trawler built at Beverley in Yorkshire in 1937 for the Kingston (upon Hull) Steam Trawling Company. In September 1939, along with 66 other trawlers she was taken over by the Royal Navy, first as an armed boarding vessel then as an anti-submarine vessel. She was fitted with a 4-inch gun and machine guns. A seaman visiting a friend on board the ship at Kirkwall was horrified to find her overrun with literally thousands of cockroaches.

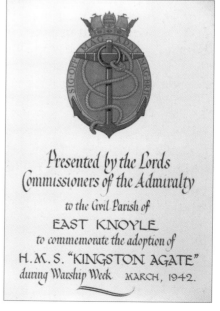

The ship was later fumigated, and earned distinction after being assigned to the 27th Auxiliary anti-Submarine Group. According to the ship's records, Kingston Agate was on the difficult and dangerous Northern Patrol when at 5.15 a.m. on April the 14th 1941 in company with sister ship Kingston Amber off St. Catherine's a German Heinkel 111 'flew from the land and passed over us with its navigation lights

*East Knoyle received this certificate from the Admiralty after adopting HMS Kingston Agate, sometimes described as 'HMT' i.e. HM Trawler, during Warship Week 1942. The neighbouring village of Sedgehill received an identical citation.*

Presented by the Lords Commissioners of the Admiralty

to the Civil Parish of

EAST KNOYLE

to commemorate the adoption of

H.M.S. "KINGSTON AGATE"

during Warship Week MARCH, 1942.

on. It wheeled and came north straight for us. We fired a short burst of .5 inch and machine gun fire. The plane passed over us again, wheeled to starboard and came at us (again) from the north. This time we attacked it heavily with good effect. The tracer was observed to enter the plane near the nose. It swerved around towards Kingston Amber's port bow, struck her top mast and eventually landed in the sea. The Kingston Amber turned to pick up survivors, and we proceeded to rendezvous with two submarines at Position 'W''. Strangely, 'the aircraft did not actually attack this ship in any way'. This was the first time that trawlers had achieved such a feat, and the Admiralty was delighted.

Captain Richard Kirby, the ship's Administrative Authority wrote a note to the Commander in Chief Portsmouth: 'I consider that the destruction of this hostile aircraft reflects great credit on all concerned' with which the C-in-C agreed: 'Noted with satisfaction', he wrote. Leading Seaman George Copperwheat in Agate and Ordinary Seaman Norman Foster in Amber were both Mentioned in Despatches, and deservedly so.

Agate was closely involved in an even more significant engagement four months later. On August the 27th, Squadron Leader Thompson RAF, coincidentally a Kingston upon Hull man, piloting his Hudson aircraft of 269 Squadron, took off from Kaldaharnes 30 miles southeast of Reyjkavik and spotted a large German submarine running on the surface 80 miles south of the Icelandic coast.

This boat was U5 70, built by Blohm & Voss in Hamburg, newly commissioned on the 15th of May 1941 and placed under the command of Leutnant Hans-Joachim Rahmlow. Having completed just one patrol, she was on a training mission when located.

*Kingston Agate and her sister ship Kingston Amber (pictured here at speed), both of the Northern Patrol, raced in worsening weather to join HMS Northern Chief. (Photograph courtesy of the Imperial War Museum, London, Negative No.A8600).*

The submarine was first seen by the Hudson's navigator. The pilot dived, and as the navigator shouted 'Now' a depth charge was released, shortly after which the plane's rear gunner saw a column of water shooting up high into the air. The U-boat then abandoned a crash dive and surfaced again rapidly. About a dozen of the crew tumbled out of the conning tower, apparently intending to man the boat's gun, so the navigator ordered the Hudson to continue firing its machine guns. Confusion followed among the U-boat crew as the aircraft made four attack runs. As it came round for a fifth attack the submarine waved a white board in surrender.

The U-boat was ordered to keep a light showing while Squadron Leader Thompson, a Catalina flying boat from 209 Squadron and other Hudson aircraft kept watch in fast worsening weather. Meanwhile an urgent call was sent out for surface craft to come to the scene. First to arrive was the armed trawler HMT Northern Chief, followed by HMT Kingston Amber and HMT Kingston

*Lieutenant Campbell and two messdeck volunteers from Kingston Agate Approach U-570. (Photograph courtesy of the Imperial War Museum, London, Negative No. C2073A).*

Agate – the first command appointment for its captain Lieutenant Henry L'Estrange RNR. Although U570 was unable to dive and running out of battery power, the newly arrived surface ships were concerned that the U-boat commander might try to scuttle his boat and abandon ship – something that would have been hazardous anyway until the seas abated. Northern Chief was taking no chances of losing the precious prize and threatened to fire on any survivors if an attempt was made to scuttle the boat before taking to the life rafts. With half a gale now blowing, Leutnant Hans Rahmlow protested in English that no scuttling or abandoning the craft was intended. Nevertheless Lt L'Estrange noticed that his own instructions to the submarine to correct its trim were not being complied with, so he also menaced it with Agate's 4-inch gun and the trim improved. After a 30 hour standoff, by which time HMS Burwell and HMCS Niagara, formerly USS Thatcher( two elderly 'Town' class destroyers passed on to the Royal Navy in response to an urgent plea from Prime Minister Winston Churchill to US President Roosevelt) had arrived together with HMT Wastwater and HMT Windermere. Once more U-570 allowed her bows to dip dangerously deep into the water, perhaps in the hopes of scuttling her. This abruptly ceased when one of the destroyers fired a burst over the conning tower. An attempt by Windermere to get a line across to the submarine was unsuccessful; but the next day, when the seas abated, Agate's First Lieutenant (Jock Campbell) and two messdeck volunteers managed it, boarding the U-boat in a Carley float. Five hours later with little or no co-operation from the Germans the sub's complement of 44 were transferred to Agate. Leutnant Rahmlow and his officers at first refused to leave the boat, but Lt L'Estrange passed word that his 4-inch gun would settle the issue unless they got into the boat 'pretty damn quick' . . . which they did.

Northern Chief towed the vessel while Agate took the crew to Iceland, where the first great benefit was secured. Priceless intelligence material was recovered by Edward Thomas RNVR, naval intelligence officer and Assistant King's Harbourmaster Hvalfjord, Iceland. He boarded the beached sub and waded through 'a filthy pap of foul smelling bilge water, diesel oil, excrement and vomit'. It seems not to have included the boat's Enigma coding machine, but its captain would have had plenty of time to throw it overboard.

The official report to the Admiralty on the action contained recommendations that the conduct of Officers and Men on Kingston Agate should be recognised. The Honours and Awards Committee, meeting on 10th October 1941 'carefully considered the claims to recognition of Officers and Men of H.M.T. Kingston Agate' and submitted that 'a letter of appreciation, mentioning the names of those particularly recommended, should be sent'. This was approved on the 13th. A letter headed 'Capture of U. 570' from the Secretary to the Admiralty to Flag Officer Commanding Iceland (C), copied to the Commanding Officer HM Trawler Kingston Agate read:

'With reference to your submission . . . of 16th September containing recommendations for Officers and Men for good service when U. 570 was captured. I am commanded by My Lords Commissioners of the Admiralty to request that you will convey to:

> Lieutenant Henry Owen L'Estrange, RNR
> Lieutenant Hector Brownlie Campbell, RNVR
> Sub Lieutenant John Wooler Wrightson, RNVR
> Leading Seaman John H Day
> Seaman Robert C Bratcher
> Seaman Gilbert McG Reid
> And Seaman Peter B Roughead

An expression of their appreciation of the courage, seamanship and devotion to duty shown by them on this occasion.

Subsequently, in the King's Birthday Honours 1942, Lt L'Estrange was awarded the Distinguished Service Cross (DSC), Lt Campbell an MBE, and the remainder 'Mentioned in Dispatches'. In the New Year Honours List 1943, Leading Seaman Albert E Smith and Telegraphist Oswin Bell were also 'Mentioned in Despatches' but no details are to hand.

*U-570, after refitting as HMS Graph, completing sea trials in Holy Loch. (Photograph courtesy of the Imperial War Museum, London, Negative No.A9874).*

Once towed across to Barrow in Furness, Lieutenants Ashe Lincoln and Martin Johnson of the Naval Directorate of Torpedoes and Mining had the hair-raising task of rendering the boat's damaged, but still live, torpedoes safe. Being unfamiliar with the new and advanced German design, they had to work very slowly and carefully, as the warheads had been armed. After a number of civilian fitters had been asked to assist but had declined, a brave young welder volunteered and wielded his blow torch under instruction so as to cut away the plating crushed on to the torpedoes. Although anonymous so far, efforts continue to be made to trace him.

The second remarkable happening was that since the boat's damage was not in fact extensive, she was refitted at Barrow and returned to service as HMS Graph, the only submarine in history to have such an experience. The First Lieutenant on board U570 when she was brought to Barrow from Iceland was 'Sam' Marriott, and he was appointed to command HMS Graph when she was commissioned into the Royal Navy. Even after that, Graph's career was not entirely without incident. She served on three war patrols. The first action took place on Trafalgar Day (21 October) 1942. The boat fired a salvo of four torpedoes at a surfaced U-boat (U-333). The torpedoes exploded after the set running time, but Graph's crew heard 'breaking up noises', the enemy submarine was classed as sunk, and Marriott received a DSO. It was not until after the war that research established that U-333 had, in fact, escaped. A couple of months later, in December 1942, while on Arctic Convoy escort duty, Graph sighted the German heavy cruiser 'Admiral Hipper' through its periscope but was unable to close within torpedo range.

On 20 March 1944, whilst in tow, the boat was wrecked on the West coast of Islay in the Hebrides. She was salvaged, but scrapped three years later, in 1947.

The German crew from U-570 became Prisoners of War. Captain Rahmlow and First Officer Bernhardt Brendt were held at Grizedale Hall in the Lake District where the senior German officer was a distinguished former U-boat commander, Otto Kreschmer. Prisoners were not allowed to hold any form of Court Martial, but resentment against the conduct of U-570's officers was bubbling. Rahmlow was transferred out of the camp, but Brendt was subjected to a 'Council of Honour' and found guilty of 'cowardice'. It so happened that before entering British service, U-570 went on show to the public at Barrow. Brendt was offered the chance to redeem himself if he could sabotage the vessel. He did manage to escape, but was shot dead by the Home Guard while evading recapture. Buried with military honours, his body was re-interred after the war in the German War Cemetery at Cannock Chase.

The noted author James Follett wrote a radio play and later a book 'The U-boat that lost its nerve' on the capture of U-570 (disguised as U-700, a non existent U-boat number, by him). To his fury, and that of many others, Universal Studios in the USA brought out a film 'U-571' at the start of this century purporting to be the story of the capture of an Enigma machine and making a mockery of both British and German history. Enigma was in fact captured from U-110 with two British servicemen losing their lives. U-571 had a distinguished record of service in the German Navy until 1944 but no Enigma machine was captured from it.

Kingston Agate survived the war, was reconverted to fishing and handed back to her owners. She was sold to Belgium in 1964 and is believed to have been scrapped.

No record has come to light of any contact between HMT Kingston Agate and her adopting parishes, but the author would be glad to receive any information to the contrary.

# 'O Praise ye the Lord'
# Primitive Methodists in Knoyle

A REVIVAL of evangelical religious thinking in the 18th Century was given form and direction by the ordained Church of England minister John Wesley. Inspired by his visit to America and the practices of the Moravian Church he toured the countryside tirelessly on horseback, praying and preaching. His preaching in Wiltshire spanned over half a century where his meetings attracted huge followings of ordinary people and were often held on farms or in the open air.

From these beginnings there developed the (Wesleyan) Methodist movement which continues as a worldwide religious organisation, but which as it became more structured alienated some who felt that the fervently expressed, passionate faith of the original Methodist evangelists was being sacrificed to order and conformity.

Those who felt this most strongly included many poor people whose lives had been disrupted by the agricultural and industrial revolutions: Farm labourers made landless and jobless in the wake of farming changes such as the Land Enclosures which replaced the time-honoured but inefficient strip field system where a farmer might have strips in fields scattered throughout the parish. There were also migrants from the country to the towns and cities where employment in mills, mines and factories might provide companionship and a regular wage, but be bought at the price of domestic squalor, filth and appalling working conditions.

Under the leadership of Hugh Bourne and William Clowes on the borders of Cheshire and Staffordshire 'Primitive' Methodism was born with 'Camp Meetings' – the first at Mow Cop on May the 31st 1807, beginning at 6 a.m. . This was, by all accounts a remarkable scene, with prayer groups in abundance, preachers testifying from improvised pulpits, and the singing of hymns. A more organised and very successful event was held at the same spot two months later. Early Primitive Methodists often followed a daytime open air meeting with a love feast in a barn in the evening.

By now, the regular Methodists were becoming alarmed, and though the new tendency had no wish to leave, its members were shortly afterwards expelled for their unorthodox spreading of the Gospel. The new denomination took the title 'Primitive Methodists', with their first chapel being built at Tunstall in North Staffordshire.

In Wiltshire, the initiative for the building of Primitive Methodist chapels stemmed from the Wiltshire Mission, begun by William Heath in the 1830's when the Wesleyan Methodist influence was lessening. First to be built was Brinkworth, between Malmesbury and Wootton Bassett, then to Swindon and North Wiltshire, down the eastern county border and finally from Salisbury westward along the Ebble and Nadder valleys. By 1850 180 such chapels had been registered, and according to the Salisbury Diocese 'Register of Certified Dissenters' Meeting Houses' a chapel was built at The Green for Primitive Methodists in 1843. Its early years show a healthy number in the congregation, for in 1851 90 and 79 are recorded as attending afternoon and evening services – many will, no doubt have been present at both. The East Knoyle chapel was administered as part of the Shaftesbury and Gillingham Circuit under a Superintendent Preacher, who in 1875 was the Reverend Thomas Powell of Gillingham. There were Primitive Methodist chapels in at least 14 other nearby locations including: Shaftesbury, Cann, Enmore Green, Gillingham, Penselwood, Stour Provost, Zeals, Mere, Alvediston, Buckhorn Weston, Hindon, Kington Magna and Motcombe. The 'Prims' or 'Ranters' as they were known – the latter nickname borrowed from a 17th Century denomination famous for their declamatory style of worship and used because of the 'Prims' habit of singing in the streets – maintained a separate existence until 1932, when the then 200,000 members joined the Wesleyans and the United Methodists to form a unified Methodist Church.

The Primitive Methodists' first recorded services in Knoyle were in 1843, though there is an unresolved riddle about the 'chapel' mentioned above – as its exact location is unclear. The land for the present building was purchased for the quite considerable sum of £30 just three years later in 1846, which is strange. In 1857, the existing building of the Ebenezer Primitive Methodist chapel opened its doors for worship. The late Mr Albert Wyndham ('Bob') Fletcher recalled that it was built with bricks from the village brickworks. These would have been fired in the kiln which was situated in Underhill by the road from the crossroads on Windmill Hill leading towards West Knoyle. The brickmaker was John Ford, presumably with the assistance of 20 year old George Ford, described in the 1871 census as a 'Brickfields Labourer'.

The name 'Ebenezer' literally means 'Stone of Help' in Hebrew and refers to the time when the Israelites asked Samuel to intercede for them with God so that they might not again be defeated by the Philistines, who had killed four thousand men in an earlier encounter – and had carried away the Ark of the Covenant. The Lord listened and 'thundered with a mighty voice' which 'threw the Philistines into confusion' a situation rapidly exploited by the men of Israel who went on to complete the rout. Samuel then took a stone and set it up at the battlefield saying 'Thus far the Lord has helped us'. This was clearly felt to be a suitable dedication for the new chapel.

There was a single door in the middle of the north side, facing a pulpit at the far end. The pulpit had space on the southeast side to accommodate visiting preachers. Music was provided (latterly at least) by a harmonium with eleven stops. The decoration was plain. The 1910 Internal Revenue 'Domesday' survey describes the interior as 'very plain – deal furnishing and dado, distempered walls above the dado and a small moveable pipe organ' (which must have been removed at a later date). At that time the Methodist Council valued the property at £380, which the Inland Revenue noted as 'very high – should be £250'.

A list of Chapel House Trustees shows that they were drawn not only from the village but from quite far afield. In 1847, just six are recorded, of whom only one, Labourer Thomas Merchant, was from the village. In 1884 and 1948, the numbers had swollen to 16 and 19 respectively made up as follows:

| | 1884 | 1948 |
|---|---|---|
| Baker & Confectioner | | 1 |
| Blacksmith | 1 | 1 |
| Civil Servant | | 1 |
| Coal Merchant | | 1 |
| Decorator | | 1 |
| Labourers | 7 | 2 |
| Dairy Farmers | 1 | 2 |
| Dairyman | 1 | |
| Electrical Engineer | | 1 |
| Engine Driver | 1 | |
| Farmer | 1 | 1 |
| Fitter | | 1 |
| Roadman | | 2 |
| Glazier | 1 | |
| Insurance Agent | 1 | |
| Jeweller | | 1 |

| | |
|---|---|
| Lorry Driver | 1 |
| Pastrycook | 1 |
| Pictureframe Maker 1 | |
| Porter 1 | |
| Rating Officer (retd) | 1 |
| Schoolteacher | 1 |

The pattern of services differed markedly from that of the Church of England in particular. The calendar of most Festivals, a set list of readings and the celebration of Saints' days received little or no attention. There were however plenty of 'special' Sundays devoted to such causes as Temperance and Overseas Missions. The three great events in the Primitive Methodist year were the Chapel Anniversary, celebrated at East Knoyle in March or April, the Sunday School Anniversary in mid June and Harvest Festival in September or early October. These continued to take pride of place until the Church's last years.

Members were encouraged to take an interest in affairs in the wider world. The record for 1963 lists a number of outside speakers covering topics such as:

Mrs Ina Matthews of Milton-on-Stour talking on 'The Wind of Change in East Africa';

The Vicar of Gillingham describing his 'Wanderings in the Cities of Northern Italy';

Dr. Fawcett of Gillingham on 'My Life on Tristan da Cunha';

Mr Henry King speaking of his 'Schooldays in Pekin' and 'The Red Sea Slave Trade'.

Robust singing of hymns set to popular stirring tunes was a great feature of the call to evangelism. Typical was the hymn known as 'The Primitive Methodist Grand March' which ran: 'Hark the Gospel News is sounding. Christ has suffered on the tree, Streams of mercy are abounding, Grace for all is rich and free'.

While the Minister took the leading role in Church life, lay people played a very large part – larger indeed than in the Methodist mainstream until the reunification in 1932. For half a century, the outstanding figure in the East Knoyle's Primitive Methodist Church's work was Mr Reginald Lampard.

Born on 25 October 1896, Reginald was determined to volunteer for service at the outbreak of World War I, and enlisted in the Royal Marines as soon as he could after his 18th birthday. He took part in the terrible events of the Gallipoli campaign against the Turks in 1915. This was designed to capture the then Turkish capital of Constantinople (Istanbul) and to create safe southern sea links to our Imperial Russian allies.

Faulty planning, incompetent execution and atrocious front line conditions doomed the expedition to ultimate disaster. Death was a constant companion, and Reginald suffered a sharp reminder of this when he volunteered to be the first to move from his trench which was coming under heavy enemy fire. Although he did not discover it until later, the rifle he was using (which was not his own) could not be fired. Nevertheless he survived unscathed; though his comrades were killed one by one by the enemy sniper overlooking their position. With stinking corpses littering the battlefield and a generally insanitary environment; enteric fever, dysentery and diarrhoea were rampant. The Allies lost over 140,000 dead and wounded. For Reginald Lampard, the experience left a deep-seated realisation of the horrors of war, which was to come back to haunt him. This awareness deepened when he was later posted to the Western Front and fell victim to a German gas attack, with serious effects. Although undoubtedly qualified to receive the three campaign medals, known to the soldiers as 'Pip, Squeak and Wilfred': The 1914 Star, the British War Medal (1914-1916) and the Victory Medal, Reginald did not apply.

After the Armistice in November 1918, as he sought to pick up the threads of his life, there grew a determination to use his best efforts to work for peace based upon his strengthened Christian values.

On demobilisation, he sought to become a Church of England Lay Reader but his application was not successful. Undeterred by this setback he applied to the Primitive Methodists. This time he was duly appointed, and so (supported by his wife Elsie) began a long period of stalwart service, until eventually illness curtailed his activities. He was Chapel Steward and organist – indeed at home there were no less than three instruments, eventually smashed in the postwar years before the days of 'The Antiques Road Show' with its appreciation of the value of Bygones.

*Left to right: Nina Roberts, Mrs. Elsie Lampard Mr. Reginald Lampard, the sister of the bride at a family wedding.*

Listed as a 'Roadman' in the 1948 Trustees list, Reginald was Superintendent of the Sunday School, with weekly instruction leading up to the Annual Anniversary service and an annual coach trip to the seaside at Weymouth for children and their parents, arranged by him and eagerly looked forward to by the children. There was never an empty seat and sometimes two coaches were hired. The coach park in the town always had a fair and – as one eyewitness recalls: 'It was a nightmare to get the children to leave!'

As a young neighbour of the Chapel, Mrs Ruby Jay remembers: 'All of us children up at The Green went to Sunday School at 2 o'clock taken by Mr Lampard. Afterwards he used to take us for a walk in the woods to look at the flowers or to gather nuts in season. We then went home for our tea, after which it was time to go back to the Chapel for Evening Service. My aunt, Doris Fry was the organist'. The pedals had to be worked to produce the music, but it may be that there was also a lever at the side to operate the blower.

Even as late as 1970, just four years before the Chapel closed, he continued to take a practical interest in church affairs. The Annual meeting of Church Trustees in that year recorded their thanks to him for paying for interior decorating, at a time when finances were becoming very stretched. Reginald was laid to rest on 20 December 1973, the burial service being conducted by the Reverend Edith Young, last Pastor of the United Reformed Church at the other end of the village.

It is an indication of the improvement in relations between the Church of England and Nonconformist denominations since Victorian times that the Reverend Basil Palmer, Rector of St. Mary's, should write in the Parish Magazine: 'Reggie was a true Christian whose simple faith was as sincere as it was steadfast. We do not see many like him today and the village is the poorer for his passing'.

In the main, the story of the last days as chronicled in the record of Trustees' meetings makes sad reading. In 1961, the caretaker, Mrs Mock, was asked to consider giving her services free of charge – but on the understanding that she would receive a gift of equal value in lieu of pay. This was because the Trustees had found out that they were 'legally obliged to pay National Insurance, but not if there was no salary'. It seems that this was put into effect, without objection from government bureaucracy! At the same time the chapel was redecorated by voluntary labour, with the Trust buying the materials.

By 1962, the number of members had shrunk to seven, but they were not prepared to give in without taking steps to try and halt the decline. It was agreed to try to start a meeting for fellowship on Thursday afternoons and Mr Lampard and the meeting expressed their willingness to visit house-to-house, inviting people to join.

In the same year it was agreed to invite Mr T.G. Mounte of the Caravan to Village Children's Mission to conduct a mission in East Knoyle (the outcome is not recorded). In 1965, the report on two cherished activities (The Family Circle and the Sunday School) was gloomy if not actually despairing: 'Despite many valiant efforts, there seemed little to show for our work, but all the same we are sure that the work must continue'.

*Ebenezer Chapel interior in 1975.*

*The Chapel back garden in need of attention.*

In 1970, by which time annual Trustee Meetings were being held at Hindon, chaired by the Minister there, interior redecorating done for what turned out to be the last time, paid for by Mr Lampard as mentioned above. Caretaker Mrs Mock's sons – described as 'The Mock Boys' were asked to clear the vegetation and clean out the gutters. In a final flourish a new notice board was ordered which remained in place to the end.

The decision to close came just four years later. The record at the final Trustees' Meeting on 20 October 1974 stated: 'As services had ceased some months previously and there was now only one member, it was decided that the property should be sold after the removal of any contents needed elsewhere'. The Trustees did, however, place restrictions on the building's use. No religious services were to be held without the

*The Chapel's last days, awaiting sale in 1975.*

written consent of the Methodist Church. Furthermore, the premises were not to be used for the manufacture, sale or distribution of intoxicating liquor, as a public dance hall, or for gambling.

The sale went ahead. The new owners have researched its past, and lavished great care on the property, which continues as a private residence. Thus came to an end over 130 years of Christian endeavour in supporting a set of beliefs that made an enduring mark on England's religious life and continues within the Methodist movement today.

# Damascus in Knoyle

H OW DID A HIGH CLASS mid-Victorian building with strong oriental influences come to take shape as a village school in East Knoyle? The answer contains some surprising twists, involving a number of the most eminent names in artistic society.

From the early 18th century until 1838, education for the village children was provided through the charities set up by the Rector the Reverend Charles Trippett in 1707 and by Mary, the widow of his successor the Reverend John Shaw – the latter admitting pupils from the age of three. In 1765, the Trippett capital was reinvested in two securities of the Fisherton (Salisbury) Turnpike Road Trust at 5%.

In 1808 this system catered for 26 children and ten years later there were four other day schools teaching a total of 65 pupils.

The Charity Commissioners in their report on East Knoyle covering the period from 1812 noted that in 1837 there was no schoolhouse belonging to the parish. However, Patience Brockway, an uncertificated teacher, who had been appointed schoolmistress in 1812 (she also discharged the duties of Sunday School teacher) taught two dozen pupils in her own house, which she rented from the Rector. Reading and writing were taught to all the children, with girls also receiving instruction in needlework. Patience received the £5 interest as salary for many years. The lease of her cottage, which stood on the corner of The Street and Church Road was a 'lease for lives' she being the sole survivor of the contract. Successive rectors had refused to grant a new lease, as they wanted to ensure that the property would remain available to be used as a schoolhouse after her death.

In fact, in the next year (1838) a purpose-built school was built a few yards closer to the church, using funds raised by public subscription. Patience Brockway was schoolmistress, and Mr. John Tanswell was in post as headmaster not later than 1848, and possibly much earlier. Although a stern figure of authority in his black tail coat bound with braid, he had a somewhat 'curious sidling walk and an upper lip as long as the one given to Bradlaugh in caricatures'. He served the school faithfully for 40 years and more and was widely respected. His school logbook gave few clues as to his personality, but he must have been a skilful negotiator to maintain his position successfully while working under the eye of strong, diverse characters such as the Rector, Canon Milford, Alfred Seymour, owner of Knoyle House and later on The Hon. Percy Wyndham who bought the Clouds estate on the hill from Mr Seymour and developed it into a national social and cultural centre. The Rector's daughter Violet, who recorded village events in her diaries and her privately published book on the village, worked with both Mr Tanswell and his assistant Miss Minns,

*Patience Brockway's cottage (on left) and the National School, 1845 (from a Sepia colour wash by Jane Bouverie of Knoyle House).*

who was appointed in 1881. When he died in 1891, she wrote 'the description of him as a good, worthy man would not be an overstatement'. She was a perceptive lady and as an epitaph it would have been very accurate.

The 1838 National School was just a few steps up the slope from Patience Brockway's cottage. The 70 to 80 children were all taught in one schoolroom by John Tanswell and Patience Brockway, with the help of two pupil teachers. According to the Warburton Census of Wiltshire schools, there was a private school at this time, taught by a schoolmistress, the pupils being 'twenty children of farmers and trades people'.

A national milestone was reached with the passing of the 1870 Elementary Education Act by the Liberal Government led by William Gladstone. This laid down the foundations of our national public education system at elementary level. In East Knoyle, although the discipline and standard of instruction in the National School were assessed as 'very fair', the cramped accommodation did not meet the new government criteria. Two important sections of the Act were to present great difficulties for the Rector, who was determined that the school should receive religious education from him, in accordance with the practices of the Church of England ('C of E'). The first was that if a School Board was constituted and finance provided from the 'Rates' (which in recent times have been rebranded as 'Council Tax') no parliamentary grant from the Privy Council could be given if religious teaching followed a particular denomination. Therefore if the religious education in a voluntary school was C of E there would be no help from public money.

Furthermore, if a government grant were to be provided, the amount coming to the National School would depend on what other schooling might be provided in the parish. In the case of East Knoyle, there had been A 'British School' since 1854, built by the silk manufacturer Mr. Jupe of Mere for the children of the village Congregational nonconformist community. It was sited next to the Congregational church – usually known informally as 'The Chapel'. A polite but stiffly worded request from the Rector to the Congregational Pastor for details of school capacity and pupil numbers received a courteous reply, ending with; 'Trusting that in this great movement we shall be actuated with a desire to glorify God and bless our generation'.

The stage was now set for Mr. Tanswell's National School to undergo a transformation. The progress and outcome of the project was to be determined by the interaction of four factors – all with the initial letter 'P': Personalities, Perceptions, Politics and the British fiscal units in 1870 and for the next century of Pounds, Shillings and Pence.

The artistic inspiration came from Sir Frederick (later 'Lord') Leighton, at a time when in some artistic circles Moorish and Arab influences were becoming less fashionable and giving way to those from China and Japan. He remained fascinated with the Near Eastern artistic approach: prompting travels to Turkey, especially Constantinople (later to be known as Istanbul), Egypt and Syria – as he sought inspiration for his forthcoming set of paintings.

His visits to the last two were a little out of the ordinary. In 1868, with the benefit of support from the Prince of Wales (later King Edward VII), Leighton cruised up the Nile in the luxury of a steamer with a French chef and an Italian waiter in attendance, all provided by the Viceroy of Egypt, Ismail Pasha. Further encouragement in Near Eastern studies came through an association with Richard Francis Burton, later to be styled 'Captain Sir Richard Francis Burton, Knight of the Order of St. Michael and St. George, Fellow of the Royal Geographical Society'. His entry in the encyclopedia 'Wikipedia' puts things very concisely: 'He was an explorer, translator, writer, soldier, orientalist, ethnologist, linguist, poet, hypnotist, fencer and diplomat'. As a young officer commissioned into the East India Company's Bengal Army, he obtained leave and among other adventures became one of the first Europeans to make a pilgrimage to Mecca, a dangerous mission for which he trained and prepared himself carefully, posing as a Muslim physician. In the early 1870's he was serving as the British Consul in Damascus. There he acquired for Leighton a vast array of antique artifacts, to which Leighton added when he himself visited the Syrian capital in 1873, just after Burton had left. One of Leighton's most celebrated paintings 'Old Damascus, Jews' Quarter 1873' was a direct result of his visit.

A number of paintings exist of Richard Burton, but there is one in particular which gives a striking insight into his complex character. It is a small watercolour from a private collection, hung at the Tate Britain's exhibition 'Lure of the East – British Orientalist Painting' during the summer of 2008. The portrait shows a dark, saturnine, brooding figure with piercing blue eyes, obviously at home in Arab dress (unlike many of the figures elsewhere in the gallery who appear to be in Arab fancy dress). His body language, brilliantly captured as he stands in front of his kneeling camel, exudes determination and willpower. The artist was the Pre-Raphaelite painter Thomas Seddon, (1821-1856) an admirer of Holman Hunt, profoundly affected by his extended visit to the Near and Middle East in 1854.

When travelling in Italy, Leighton met George Aitchison (Junior) for the first time. This led to a professional association and a lifelong personal friendship. Young George had been trained by his father and at London University as an architect, and became a partner in 1859. He was to become Professor of Architecture at the Royal Academy of Arts in 1887, and was elected President of the Royal Institute of British Architects in 1896. He specialized in interior design and was commissioned to design Leighton's house in Holland Park Road, London. In 1870, Aitchison was called upon to provide a pair of windows for that house. In her ground-breaking study of the East Knoyle School, Elisabeth Darby has demonstrated the striking similarity between these designs and the windows built into the school a couple of years later. It is a fair working assumption that Aitchison modified his Holland Park design for the school project.

Aitchison's connexion with the School came about through Alfred Seymour. A descendant of Henry VIII's Queen Jane Seymour, his branch of the family lived at Knoyle House and Trent, once in Somerset but now in Dorset. Besides being a landowner and lawyer, in 1870 he was a Wiltshire MP representing Salisbury, a railway entrepreneur, a gambler and a man of fashion. He was also a man with artistic knowledge and sensibility and a careful curator of the notable family portrait collection at Knoyle House, which included one of the 'Holbein' quartet of full length portraits of Henry VIII.

As Alfred's Knoyle House Game Book dutifully records, he was widely travelled, especially in the years before his marriage in 1866. Winters were partly spent abroad. Sojourns in France, Italy, Spain and Russia, were followed in 1855 with an extended tour of Egypt, the Holy Land, Constantinople, the Crimea, Montenegro, Venice and Hungary. This may have been the time when he purchased the damascened brassware noted by Elisabeth Darby and recorded in a Knoyle House inventory now in the Wiltshire and Swindon History Centre.

How Alfred came to be aware of George Aitchison is not documented, but with his London town house in Eaton Square, this was no great distance from Leighton's Holland Park residence, which was becoming a magnet to an up and coming artistic community, to become known as the Holland Park Circle, with which Aitchison practising his profession from Muscovy Court in the City of London was familiar.

Another possibility is through Aitchison's work for Lord Richard Grosvenor at Stalbridge over the Dorset border from Knoyle. Lord Stalbridge (as Richard Grosvenor later became) is mentioned in Rector Milford's daughter's diaries as

*'Old Damascus, The Jewish Quarter 1873', by Frederick Leighton (reproduced by kind permission of Mr Michael F Price and the Royal Academy of Arts – of which Leighton was elected President in 1887).*

quite frequently in Knoyle. When Alfred died in 1888, of apoplexy after a decade of ill health with chronic bronchitis, Knoyle House was let furnished to Lord Stalbridge, an indication that he was known to and trusted by the executors.

A final possibility comes through Isabella, (the second daughter of Sir Baldwin Leighton) who became Alfred's wife in 1866. Described as 'sprightly and practical-minded', she was the widow of Sir Beriah Botfield, a wealthy Member of Parliament but a pedantic snob. Sir Beriah made a hobby of studying family pedigrees. He fondly imagined that he was related to Lord Bath's family of Thynne through their ancestors, the Botvilles. Lord Bath's view on his claim is not recorded, but Ulster King of Arms comprehensively demolished Sir Beriah's research.

Alfred Seymour was in many ways the most attractive personality of the Knoyle branch of the family. There is every indication that he came to love Isabella dearly in the 22 years of their marriage. He certainly made sure that she got a welcome on approaching Knoyle by way of the London train to neighbouring Semley. As the Western Gazette recorded: 'On Tuesday 18 August Mr. A Seymour brought home his bride to Knoyle and the village and neighbourhood were consequently the scenes of great excitement. There was a plentiful display of flags at Semley station and a troop of horsemen, splendidly mounted, tenants on the Knoyle estate, and friends, were drawn up beside a triumphant arch to welcome the happy pair. The mounted gentlemen accompanied the carriages from Semley station to Knoyle, three miles distant, and all along the road there were signs of the goodwill of the inhabitants who had displayed great taste in the erection of the arches, and decking their windows with flowers. Bouquets were thrown to the bride as she passed. On arrival at Knoyle, nearly the whole population, about 1200, were assembled, the bells pealed merrily and the farmers and labourers afterwards sat down to dinner.'

In expressions of welcome to Mrs. Seymour, the hope was expressed that she would come to love the village of her new home. She clearly took this to heart.

Her late husband's will written in almost impenetrable English by Sir Beriah, had taken a lot of sorting out, but in the end it left Isabella very comfortably off – and, like Alfred, she was very willing to support worthwhile local causes, right up to the time of her death.

Alfred was very stricken by the death of his mother in 1869, after several years lingering with dropsy. He let the shooting at Knoyle House for three years to Admiral Tryon, but still kept an active interest in the village.

Rector Milford wrestled with the competing needs of finance from central government (through the Privy Council) and providing what he felt to be acceptable religious education in the new school. 'I am informed '(he wrote to Alfred Seymour)' that there must be 'no religious catechism or religious formulary which is distinctive of any particular denomination' . . . 'which would prevent me from taking my part in the religious education of the school . . . and certainly considerably impair my usefulness there'. In an effort to end on a more cheerful note, he thanked Alfred 'for a magnificent haunch of venison', which 'we with Admiral Tryon, Mr. Hall and the Troyte Bullocks did ample justice to'. In the event, the Rector 'dispensed with aid from the Privy Council' and set about raising the funds by self-help locally. The Salisbury and Winchester Journal noted that the fundraising project had been taken up heartily in the village, and was greatly promoted by the very handsome donation of £500 towards the building fund from Mr. Alfred Seymour MP.

The choice of architect was central to successful completion of the project. Alfred recommended George Aitchison. The Rector wrote on 3 November 1870 to him, inviting him to supply plans, after visiting the site noting: 'I understand that you are often now in our neighbourhood at Stalbridge'. Thus began an ultimately fruitful association, but one which must have tried Aitchison's patience quite sorely. At one stage, the Rector suggested the building be built of brick, which Aitchison said he would do if Milford was 'fully determined'. The Rector later changed the plans, more than once it seems. He also felt it would be good to have a cross placed against the school roof to which Aitchison replied that it would be better for Mr. Seymour to have the cross made into a weathervane and stuck up in a tree or over the stables of his own house. 'It will look on the schools almost as appropriate as a cow with a side pocket !' Aitchison's inclusion of Near Eastern influences never seems to have been an issue, although the Rector and the Salisbury Journal labelled them as 'Byzantine' rather than Islamic.

With Leighton as his artistic patron and Seymour's support, Aitchison felt free to design orientalism into the new school – although his principled opposition to following historical concepts too slavishly enabled him to maintain an individual approach to his work.

After the Schools' Inspectorate endorsed the need for the new school in 1870, events at first moved fast. Alfred gave ground for the new school on part of his kitchen garden – but far enough away for the noise of boisterous schoolchildren to be out of earshot. In September, the Rector and others measured out the ground, and two months later there was a meeting of ratepayers to discuss the plans for the new schools (infants and primary). The actual plans did not reach the village until a fortnight later, after which there was a delay of over a year, during which time there seems to have been little real progress – although fundraising continued apace, supported by local gentry, farmers and a number of village residents.

As a costcutting measure, Alfred sent the Rector tracings of a modification 'to cut out the stone mullions altogether, and have oak frames for the windows which would not open with sashes but like French windows'. 'I am not sure' he wrote, 'that mullions at any time, however well they may look from the outside, are ever good things; as windows never fasten well with them and the iron frames...are always getting out of order'. Aitchison did redesign the south facing windows in oak which remain today, together with an opening system hinged half way up the window, an innovation of which he may have been the originator, and which is to be seen in modern Velux roof windows.

The Rector chose as contractors Messrs Doddington and Farthing of Mere, and was in May 1872 congratulated by Aitchison on arranging to 'get the work done at such a low rate' adding 'I hope that they do their work well and have well-trained staff'.

Meanwhile, HM Inspectorate became impatient, and their report of March 1872 did not mince matters: 'It is imperative that the new premises be commenced without delay. The present room is quite inadequate'. They did not have much longer to wait for the foundation stone was laid three months later, on Midsummer's Day.

There was a large assemblage of the villagers, and the schoolchildren were formed in a semicircle around the stone. After a service led by the Rector and a hymn sung by the children, Mrs. Seymour laid the stone, which she did in a 'truly workmanlike manner'. Her husband addressed the children, stressing the importance of religion in education and that trusting in God, He would give them grace to become good men and women and to do their duty in the station in which it had pleased Him to place them. Mr. Seymour urged the parents to do their duty towards the children and towards God. In words which may have irritated the Rector and his family who were all Conservatives in politics, he reminded them that the education of children was to become a portion of 'the necessities of the state' and they should remember that they were all 'particles of that one great system which imparted knowledge throughout the whole country'.

The Rector then presented Mrs. Seymour with a silver trowel 'of chaste design', bearing within a wreath of leaves the inscription 'Presented to Mrs. Seymour, by the Rev. R.N. Milford, rector, Thomas Stacey, J.R. Gray churchwardens, and other subscribers to the East Knoyle National School, in remembrance of her having laid the first stone on 24 June 1872'. Mrs. Seymour replied that 'It is a very pretty trowel indeed, and I am exceedingly obliged to you. It is a beautiful present and it will always agreeably remind me of this day.' After three cheers for Mr. and Mrs. Seymour and Mr. and Mrs. Milford, the children were marched up to the rectory and given buns. They went down to the (old) school

*Aitchison's East Window, funded by a £50 donation from Mrs. Alfred Seymour.*

and 'were again feasted', and given the afternoon off. The Rector and his wife entertained a large party to an elegant lunch at the rectory. In welcoming Mrs. Seymour, the Rector sang the praises of Knoyle; the scenery of which was hardly to be excelled in any part of England that he had seen. Finally he thanked the Churchwardens and spoke of the hearty support he had received from them and other parishioners in the school project.

As the new building took shape, people marvelled at the pierced stone designs of the east and west windows, as already mentioned almost certainly derived from Aitchison's design drawings for Leighton House. These are reminiscent of houses in Syria and throughout the Near East, though not so often executed in stone. Mrs. Seymour gave £50 – a considerable sum in 1872 – to pay for them. On the south side the pillars and casements are styled in Near Eastern fashion, although the capitals on either side of the front door, which are in Caen stone, appear to be classically inspired. Tisbury and Ham Hill stone were also used.

*The Village School c1950.*

Funding continued to be a worry, fully recognized by George Aitchison. After pointing out that his draughtsman had had to make 20 to 30 drawings in the course of the project, and that he had already subscribed £2 to the schools, he added: 'But as I know that you clergymen have often to subscribe to these schools out of all proportion to your income, you may deduct a further £8 from what is due to me'. At the formal opening of the school by Mr. Seymour less than a year later, on 6 June 1873, the Rector made a special point of the fact that the project could not have been completed without Mr. Seymour, who had liberally borne the greater part of the financial burden. In his own speech, Mr. Seymour foresaw a school being built in every parish in the kingdom, and compulsory education made universal. 'No,No', cried Mrs. Milford. Undeterred, Alfred went on to say that he thought it would be a very good thing for the whole country. The system which had been regarded by many excellent people as an unmitigated evil, would be looked upon with favour . . . if fairly tried. He assured his hearers that all undertakings that had for their object the benefit of the inhabitants would always find him ready to give a helping hand.

The Rector based his and his wife's objection on the scenario that if a parent complained that his wages would not support compulsory education, to which he was required to contribute, he could not see magistrates fining parents for not sending their children to school.

Harmony was restored as the Rector concluded by proposing the health of Mr. Aitchison. Not over generously perhaps, he referred to the favourable comments passed on the style of the school.

# 'Emily'

IN THE 1880s times were hard for those at the bottom of the social scale. Emily was the child of socially deprived parents living in Warminster. In addition her father, Edward aged 47, was unable to speak or to hear, there were problems with alcohol and her grandmother's house was too small to provide a home for Emily and her family. Thus the family had no settled home, the two girls having been in the Warminster workhouse four times: once for 14 weeks, once for seven weeks and twice for a few days. The Parish, as the Poor Law Authority, paid for their schooling at The Hall Girls' School in the town, where they were both in Standard 1. They attended Sunday School at the parish church from time to time.

Emily led a wretched existence – so miserable that Canon Milford's daughter Beatrice wrote from her father's rectory ten miles away in East Knoyle to the Waifs and Strays Society (now the Children's Society) in London to see if they could help. A formal application for assistance was made out by Sister Mary of St. Denys House. She was a member of a recently founded Church of England religious order of nuns under the Bishop of Salisbury's jurisdiction. The Order was originally set up to carry out missionary work, both at home and abroad.

Fortunately, Beatrice Milford was not to be put off easily and as the Knoyle Waifs and Strays representative used every means at her disposal to rescue Emily from a life of despair and continuing degradation. Her letter to the London HQ of the Waifs & Strays was starkly explicit: 'She comes', Beatrice wrote 'from a terribly drunken home, or rather surroundings, for she has no home. Her father, a deaf and dumb drunkard, has forsaken her, and her mother is very drunken too'. In fact, Emily had a brother, Jim, and an elder sister Mary Jane. Mrs Torrance of Norton House , Warminster in correspondence with the Waifs and Strays wrote that the children's cases 'were piteous'; but that the Society's suggestion that she and Sister Mary should find money to contribute to the girls' care posed a problem. There were many people out of work in the area which

*Emily (Mrs. Pierce nee Haines) with her brother Jim in later life.*

had drained the charity funds. Although the Society had campaigned on the family's behalf for a long time, the parents were disapproved of by local people, who preferred to donate their money to those whom they felt were the 'deserving poor'.

The family's house (presumably meaning grandmother's overcrowded cottage) had recently been raided by the police on sanitary grounds and the children driven out. There was no possibility of the family finding a place to stay, and both girls had been living rough. Mary had been previously looked after by a relation who had died, and up to that time had been 'an attractive girl' and a 'tidy, quiet child'. Now 'she was learning evil apace and a delay would be absolutely fatal to her'. The Society wrote to Lady Halifax, formerly Lady Agnes Courtenay, daughter of the 11th Earl of Devon seeking her help. This lady agreed to take Mary into the rather forbidding- sounding Kenton Industrial Home which she had founded near the Halifax family seat at Powderham Castle in Devon. No one seemed to worry about the psychological effect of separating the two sisters, and Mary was sent off to the Home, on payment of four shillings (20p) a week. Further information about her is sparse; but she went out into service as an under housemaid on 19 December 1891. It is also known that she married Herbert Newberry on 13 February 1896.

For Emily, help was to come closer to hand. In 1888, a small cottage Waifs and Strays Home for just seven children was set up in a cottage at The Green in the village, with Annie Hayward as Matron, the (presumably Common Law) wife of

Charles Ricketts, a gardener who had been unable to work for some time due to a hip complaint. Annie appears to have been born in Watlington, Oxfordshire and lived with her mother. Before she married, she had been for 14 years in service with one family as nursery maid, and then as nurse. After their marriage Charles and Annie are recorded as living in Trent, then in Somerset but now in Dorset, where Alfred Seymour of Knoyle House had a substantial family property. This could be a significant connexion.

*Powderham Castle, Devon, the home of Lady Halifax; near to The Kenton Industrial Home where Mary Haines was sent.*

*Deepmoor Cottage at The Green, a possible location of the Waifs and Strays Cottage Home at which Emily was the first child to come under Annie Ricketts' care as Matron.*

The first arrival at the Home, on May the 18th 1888, was eight year-old Emily. Beatrice Milford's account states that she was 'in a deplorable condition, miserably dressed, not too clean, with no outfit of any kind, and shocking wounds on one foot. She also had swollen glands, and for two or three days had to stay in bed, with a doctor attending her'. However, within a short period, 'the loving care which the child has received has already done wonders for her, and she is very bright and happy, most unlike the sad little creature she was when she first came'. The children's community, at first just Emily and the Ricketts' own daughter Janet soon grew with the addition first of seven year-old Fanny from Stepney – another resilient ' sharp, quick child', followed by Ada, Maud and Alice. By all accounts they were a happy and well cared for bunch who enrolled at the new village school.

Each school day they made the threeequarter mile journey back and forth across Windmill Hill to the school. At midday, they all trooped off to the servants' hall at the Rectory to eat a packed lunch. In the summer when the weather was fine, they would play in the rectory grounds until time to return to the school room. Ada, the eldest girl, kept a careful eye on them acting as a 'little mother'. The schoolmistress herself used to remark how well behaved and obedient they were. The summer holidays seem to have been happy times for the children too, although Beatrice Milford's article for the October 1889 edition of the Waifs and Strays Newsletter makes it clear that it was not all free time: 'Mrs Ricketts very wisely keeps them employed during part of every day, so that they enjoy their play all the more. Three of them have made themselves 'Sunday pinafores', after the work was cut out and placed for them. September was blackberrying time, with the harvest being particularly good in 1889. The children 'picked so well that Mrs Ricketts has made many pots of jam for the winter. In addition to this the children have supplied an old neighbour with enough blackberries for her to make jam'. Beatrice could not resist adding: 'They are learning to carry out the teaching of Mrs Charlesworth's delightful story', and to be 'ministering children'.

There were occasional instances of children's natural parents seeking to maintain contact with girls in the Home. The children did receive visits from their families when they were in the Home, but they were not usually permitted to go out to visit them as so many had come from what were undesirable surroundings and it was felt that they needed a completely fresh start away from bad influences. In Emily's case her mother Sarah did write letters to Emily and Beatrice sought guidance on whether Emily should be allowed to go home for a night. Beatrice's view was that she would be reluctant to part with Emily as she feared that her mother would not allow her to return to Knoyle – as Sarah was reckoned to regard the Home 'as a prison'. The reply is not recorded, but the indications are that the visit did not take place.

At the start there was a Knoyle Committee appointed to be in contact with the Home and with the Waifs & Strays Society; while it was usual practice for wealthy supporters of the Society to become 'sponsors' of an individual child who would then become their protégé. In Emily's case contributors towards her maintenance were Mr F.A. Were of Gatwicke Hall, Barrow Gurney, Bristol, and Miss M.F. Blomfield of Launton Rectory, Bicester.

Shortly afterwards it was Christmas time at the Home, and while the family atmosphere could not be complete, the girls were certainly not neglected. Once more Beatrice Milford describes the scene: 'The children had a most happy Christmas, and had numerous presents. The Matron was awoke (sic) very early on Christmas morning, by sounds from one of the little girls' rooms – 'I've got a doll' cried little Alice, the youngest child. On striking a match, Mrs Ricketts found the time was only three o'clock, so she told the children they really must go to sleep again. In the morning there was great excitement; the children's stockings had been hung up, and had sweets and cards in, whilst beside them lay other presents. Mrs Hilda Chester had sent presents for all the children, with which they were most delighted; and each child (except Maud Kerridge, who cannot write) wrote a very neat little note of thanks to her. Mrs Bull sent nice presents to her two special charges, Fanny and Alice; Lady Stalbridge, after the New Year, sent up to the Home, by two of the children, a large piece of Christmas cake, which was much appreciated. Altogether, our children were not at all forgotten this Christmas time.'

Easter was another time for social activity at the Home. In 1893, Violet Milford (one of Beatrice's sisters) recorded in her diary: 'There was a Band of Hope entertainment at a quarter to eight' (put on by children from both the village and the Home). 'A large number of children and one table full of parcels . . . such a success. It was mixed dialogues and singing. The children looked so nice, were very good and did their parts excellently. Mabel Tanswell and L Wareham sang very prettily . . . Janet Ricketts as the fairy was so good . . . '

The progress in Emily's education was striking. As one example, each year an external examiner came to the school to examine the pupils in Scripture Knowledge – what would nowadays be called 'R.E'. Twice in six years Emily was picked out for special mention, duly recorded by the Rector in his monthly church magazine.

At the end of that time, a series of events was to change Emily's life once again. Canon Milford's son Humphrey got married. His father set him up as Headmaster of a new boy's school at Yockleton in Shropshire. Emily, now 14, joined the school's domestic staff. She did not, however lose all her Knoyle connexions; for Humphrey and his bride also enrolled Susan Hooper, a mature lady from the village

*A happy photograph of Emily and her daughter.*

Another happy photograph of Emily's daughter
with her daughters, the author and his dog
'George' in East Knoyle in 2006.

Annie Ricketts' gravestone.

to be the school cook. Susan in due course, became attracted to a local widower called Henry Pierce and they got married on 19 April 1900. Henry had a son also called Henry Pierce (Junior) and Emily and young Henry got married just a few months later, on 24 November. If this was a fairy story one would say 'and they lived happily ever after' . . . The full details are not known, but the author has a happy photograph of Emily with her daughter; and this lady, now in her early eighties came with her daughters to visit him in Knoyle.

As for the location of the cottage children's home, with the Children's Society having no clues apart from being a cottage in the Knoyle hamlet of The Green; Emily's family, Mr Alan Oakley from the former Primitive Methpodist Chapel and I have followed a trail of frustration – until a chance conversation with Mr Clifford Sully indicated that Deepmoor Cottage at The Green had been a Dr Barnado's home in the 1920's. We know that it housed more than one family at some time in the past. It is tempting to think that this could have been the Waifs and Strays' home location. And there, for the time being, the matter rests, while we explore the possibilities further.

Annie Ricketts died in 1900, and is buried in St. Mary's churchyard extension. At the 1901 Census, Charles was living with his daughter and two Ricketts relations. He himself died in the following year and is buried next to Annie – described in the burial register as 'Matron of the Children's Home' with the unusual epitaph 'She did what she could'. This should probably be read as a sincere tribute to her efforts to give her charges a decent start in life.

# 'Men of Iron'

UNTIL THE COMING of the motor car, the blacksmith/farrier was a central figure in village life. Many, but not all have now disappeared. In East Knoyle, there was a smithy in Milton with the blacksmith Aaron Gray.

*Mr. Aaron Gray, the blacksmith at Milton, during World War I.*

At the start of World War I, he shod all the farm and draught horses in the central and northern part of the parish and must have connived at one farmer hiding away his two splendid beasts when the Government sent round agents to commandeer as many suitable horses as they could find (and they only took the best) to ship them over to the Western Front in France, from where they were most unlikely to return amid all the slaughter.

The principal forge was, and is, in The Street. Around the turn of the 19th/20th Century the blacksmith was Mr Phillips, then came the imposing but genial Mr Tom Bath, followed in 1921 by Mr Albert

*Mr. Tom Bath, blacksmith in The Street.*

Sully who began to diversify his business. To shoeing were added first a cycle business, then motor cycles and finally a garage for motor cars (Mr Sully also ran two lorries). The forge probably dates from the 18th century though its origins could be even earlier. Mr Clifford Sully, Albert's son succeeded him, then there was Mr Lennox Kilner, and the forge is still in operation with Mr David Tomlin making high quality ornamental ironwork. The garage (latterly run by Mr and Mrs David Williams) with its petrol pumps sadly no longer exists as such ,but survives as a showroom for classic cars.

*Mr. David Tomlin, present blacksmith in The Street, at work on an ornamental gate.*

*A sad sight. The last day at Mr. and Mrs. Williams' garage.*

From 1752 to the 1870s there was a turnpike at the southern end of the village, and the keeper's cottage is still there. When the turnpike trusts ceased to function as central maintenance of the highways became established, the future of the turnpikes became problematical. Some, as at Motcombe remain as private houses, but many were demolished.

Robert Haynes and Ivor Slocombe have chronicled the fate of the Wiltshire Tollhouses. When a toll road was adopted as an open thoroughfare, The Turnpike Trusts were required to realise their assets to clear their debts, and the Act of Parliament laid down that they had first to be offered to the owners of adjoining land, literally at knockdown prices in most cases. If those owners declined, their permission was to be sought for an auction to be held. If this was refused demolition

*Motcombe turnpike, dating from 1836.*

*Primrose Cottage, once a small smithy at the turnpike, to meet the needs of wayfarers.*

*All that remained of the East Knoyle turnpike in 2005.*

was the only answer with the materials sold off. No documentary evidence of what happened at Knoyle has come to light, but as all that was found at the turnpike site when the bypass was built in 1995 was a collection of half a dozen bricks, the outcome seems pretty clear.

Just opposite the turnpike site lies Primrose Cottage, where a small smithy attended to the shoeing needs of wayfarers. It is said that the sounds of horses' hooves can still sometimes be heard in that house.

# The Forgotten Soldier

JUST ACROSS the parish boundary, in Sedgehill stands Hays, now a nursing home and retirement complex. Opposite the entrance, half hidden among undergrowth and newly planted saplings stands a 12 foot high column, with the following inscription:

TO THE GLORY OF GOD
AND IN PROUD MEMORY
OF A LOVING SON AND BROTHER
NIEL SHAW STEWART
1 RIFLE BRIGADE
KILLED IN ACTION AT
GUILLEMONT FRANCE
AUGUST 21 1916
AGED 22
R.I.P

The ancient Scottish family of Shaw Stewart came from Renfrewshire and had strong connections with the Argyll and Sutherland Highlanders.

Sir Michael Robert Shaw Stewart, 7th Baronet, married Lady Octavia Grosvenor, a daughter of the Marquess of Westminster. His heir Walter Richard became a Deputy Lieutenant for Wiltshire, married Mary Beatrice and lived in Fonthill Abbey where their two sons were brought up. The younger boy, Niel was educated at Eton where he became aware of the war clouds gathering. At the age of nineteen and a half he was gazetted a Second Lieutenant and posted into the First Battalion, The Rifle Brigade. Eleven months later he was promoted Lieutenant. After a spell with the 5th (Reserve) Battalion he returned to the 1st Battalion, served in France and was wounded in 1915. After his return to active duty, he joined 'D' Company of the 3rd Battalion and in the summer of 1916 found himself opposite the village of Guillemont. The Germans had made this into a formidable obstacle, constructing a network of tunnels, concrete gun emplacements, and interconnecting dugouts; which had made it a very hard nut to crack – one which had frustrated the Allies in repeated attacks, intended to provide some relief for the main Allied assault on the Somme.

An attack by the 3rd Battalion mounted at 4.30 p.m. on August the 18th saw three companies with 'D' on the right under the command of Captain J.H. Smith crossing no Man's Land successfully without much loss by keeping very close up to an intense artillery creeping barrage. There then followed a fierce hand to hand fight with a determined enemy garrison until the battalion's first objective was captured. The plan now was for a further advance timed for 6.30 p.m. on to a second objective codenamed 'High Holborn'. Niel's company was ordered to secure the flank facing the village, while 'A' and 'B' Companies went ahead to the objective. This move was entirely successful, with the railway station being taken and the leading companies digging in on the objective. A further advance to take a trench system named 'ZZ' was not attempted as the Brigade on the Battalion's right had been unable to move forward. According to the Rifle Brigade's regimental history: 'The casualties in comparison with the results were not heavy' but nevertheless five Battalion officers and twenty soldiers had been killed while a further six officers and one hundred and ninety four soldiers were wounded or missing.

The 3rd Battalion with a company from the 1st Battalion of the Royal Fusiliers was ordered to renew the attack, secure the remainder of High Holborn and to push on to 'ZZ' trench. The date fixed was August the 21st.

*The Memorial to Niel Shaw Stewart, on the A350 opposite Hays.*

With Captain Smith a casualty, Lieutenant Butler assumed command of D Company. Once again 4.30 p.m. was zero hour, and the enemy were waiting. The first wave of attack by the brigade in front of them withered away under the hail of fire from the defenders. Lieutenants Butler and Shaw Stewart with the Fusiliers on their right pressed ahead to 'High Holborn' but at terrible cost – all the D Company officers and three quarters of their men were mown down. Next day the attackers were temporarily relieved by troops from another division, to return to the assault at the beginning of September, when after suffering further heavy casualties Guillemont was at last taken. The Battalion lost a total on the Somme of eight officers and 67 soldiers killed with a further 12 officers and 405 soldiers wounded or missing.

*Hays, now Hays House Retirement and Nursing Home, in 2007.*

Niel lies buried in Delville Wood Cemetery, created after the Armistice by bringing together the fallen from several small cemeteries and the battlefield itself.

Niel's father was no longer alive but his mother and brother were living in Hays, Sedgehill – a comfortable 19th century mansion with its home farm attached and a modest park. They expressed their grief and their pride in a brass wall plate in Sedgehill Church and the now neglected wayside cross. The pride is evident in the short Latin quotation from the poet Horace at the base of the memorial:

'Dulce et decorum est pro Patria mori' – 'It is a sweet and glorious thing to die for one's country'.

While few people today would not deplore the tragic waste of young lives on the Western Front in the First World War, the heroism of those who risked and all too often lost their lives is not in doubt. It is a sad reflection on our sense of relative values that this moving memorial to one of the fallen should so recently have been allowed to lapse into obscurity – within the last ten years.

# Ernest Francis
# in search of his Family

I n 2006, an enquiry reached the author from Mr Ernest Francis, living in the Republic of Ireland with his family. He was seeking information about his father Percy, and other members of the family who had lived in Knoyle. Percy's father's name was Fred, his sister was Evelyn (Mrs Roberts), and the Roberts' had had a son named Brian. This was the sum total of Ernest's knowledge of his father.

Research into Census returns, Parish Records, family photographs and the recollection of Knoyle residents, pointed the way to dispersing the fog of uncertainty.

*Percy Francis with the Glee Club in the 1930s. He is the dark haired young man behind the lady sitting on the right (See Key).*

**EAST KNOYLE GLEE CLUB IN THE 1930's**

**Back row (left to right):** Mrs FORWARD, Unknown, Mrs ELLIOTT, Mrs SMALL, Mr LITTLECOTT.
**Second Row (left to right):** Mrs FORWARD, Mrs FULFORD, Mrs HYDE, Mrs TANSWELL, Mr HARRIS, Mr Gerald FORWARD, Mr Percy FRANCIS, Two Unknown, Miss GREEN.
**Third Row (left to right):** Dollie FORWARD, Joan Littlecott, Mrs SULLY, Mrs BARNES, Mrs LEVER.
**Front (left to right):** Mr FORWARD, Unknown.

The 1891 Census for East Knoyle identified George and Charlotte Francis as living in Milton, within Knoyle parish. Both had come from Gloucestershire, and George was a builder working at Clouds. They had six children. Lydia, John and Harry were born before the family came to Wiltshire. William, born in 1884 died at the age of 38, four years after the end of World War I. Next in line was Fred born in 1887, who married Louise Street in 1910.

Fred and Louise had three children. The eldest was Ernest Henry (known as 'Ernie') born in 1913. He was a shop assistant at Tuck's Stores in The Street in the 1930s and was killed in action in 1944. The youngest was Evelyn May, born in 1921

*Percy Francis served in the Army in World War II, almost certainly in the London Irish Rifles.*

or 1922. She lived in a cottage by the Turnpike, having married Arthur Roberts – who like his brother –in-law Ernie, was killed in action in World War II. Their son Brian, tragically died in a road accident in 1976. Evelyn was a notable member of the village community until her death in 2003.

The middle child was Percy Alfred, born in 1915. As a young man, he was employed as chauffeur to (The Dowager) Lady Pembroke at Knoyle House. When her widowed daughter married the 7th Earl of Wicklow and moved to Shelton Abbey, County Wicklow, Percy went to Ireland too. The palatial country house dates from the 18th and 19th Centuries and remained as the family seat until 1951, when the 8th and last Earl encountered financial difficulties and was forced to sell up. The Abbey is now an Open Prison.

It was there that Percy met and married Ernest's mother. Sadly, the marriage did not last and ended in divorce. Percy came back to England, but son Ernest (named after his uncle) had absolutely no direct contact with his father. Indeed, the only responsibility he seems to have assumed was to pay for the boy's education. Percy maintained a link with his sister Evelyn and some of the family, but he was not welcome at Evelyn's cottage on the Turnpike, which was where Percy's father Fred came to live. Being strong church people with strict moral principles, they were totally against divorce. After leaving Ireland, Percy joined the British Army. His military headdress was the 'Caubeen' and his cap badge was surmounted by a dark coloured hackle, probably green. The fact that the bonnet was sloped to the left, is a strong indication that he served in the London Irish Rifles (Territorial Army). At a late stage in World War II he was either transferred or seconded to The Intelligence Corps stationed with American forces in Bavaria. There, he met and married his second wife, Herta, who was an interpreter and the daughter of a Bavarian Count. He settled in Austria with his new family, and Ernest acquired two step sisters. Percy and Evelyn were clearly close and she kept in touch with his new family when he moved to Austria. The last time he came to England was in 1976, when he attended his nephew Brian's funeral, but kept a low profile. Percy died from a heart attack on 9 December 1981, while out on a day's shooting in Austria.

As a result of the research detailed above, Ernest, his wife, their son and grandson visited East Knoyle in March 2007. Ernest was able to visit his grandfather's houses, to see his Uncle Ernest's name on the War Memorial and to talk to a cousin of Percy's sister who had kept in touch with Percy and

*Ernest Francis with his wife, son and grandson at East Knoyle in 2007.*

with his Austrian family. Ernest was overwhelmed, saying: 'Today I have found a family!' In a final touch, Brian Roberts' widow presented him with Percy's watch, which she had had in safekeeping since her husband died. Percy's Austrian wife has two daughters, one married to an Austrian Count, and one a doctor living in England. A meeting was arranged in London, which drew further threads together – and in March 2008, Ernest and his wife travelled to Klagenfurt to meet Herta at home.

# The Gift of Charity

T HROUGHOUT the Middle Ages, the joys of salvation and the perils of damnation were almost universally accepted as unchallengeable consequences of a good or evil life – and interpreted very literally by all classes of society.

The magnificent 'Doom' painting in the nave of St. Thomas' church in Salisbury depicts these in graphic detail, and emphasises that elevated rank, even for such as bishops, gives no immunity from divine retribution. One course of action, for those who could afford it, was to pay for a priest to say Mass for your soul after your death, another to demonstrate your good intentions by practising the biblical virtue of providing for the needs of the poor. For some this took the form of building and endowing almshouses, a fair number of which, founded as far back as the 10th Century, survive to meet 21st Century needs. Probably the oldest of these is the Hospital of St. John the Baptist, which can be visited in Winchester. Its founder was the Anglo-Saxon Bishop St. Brinstan, who was born in the reign of

*The Chafyn Grove almshouses at Zeals.*

King Alfred. The nearest almshouses to Knoyle to be seen are those at Zeals, six miles to the west. They were set up in 1865 by William Chafyn Grove, in memory of his mother.

Until the Reformation, the great religious houses took a leading part in providing for the sick and the poor. The Abbesses and the nuns at Shaftesbury five miles away to the south took their responsibilities seriously for nearly seven centuries. This period began with the Abbey's foundation by Alfred the Great in A.D. 888. It ended in 1539, when Henry VIII dissolved this, the richest nunnery in the land. The buildings and contents were sold off by Sir Thomas Arundell, who had at one time served the last Abbess, Elizabeth Zouch. He had been employed as a collector of rents – and was one of the two commissioners who masterminded the closure and expulsion.

The Hospital of St. John the Baptist in Salisbury Street, functioned into the 15th Century looking after 'five poor men'. The hospital dedicated to St. Mary Magdalene in Magdalene Street may have had there a connection with lepers, bringing to mind the account of Mary coming to Jesus with an alabaster box of 'very precious ointment' and pouring it over his head. It is known that it supported 12 paupers. Thomas Scalis, a priest who died in 1532, was one of those serving

the Abbey, probably by taking services, a task which women were not permitted to perform. His grave slab (now displayed in the Abbey Museum) declares his kindness and generosity to the poor. The priest appointed by Abbess Dame Margaret St. John under an endowment made in 1492, included in addition to praying at the Lady Chapel altar, the task of giving out alms to the poor every Friday. This took place from an almonry within 'Broad Hall', which stood near to what is now a restaurant by the present Town Hall.

Public charity in Knoyle parish, as elsewhere, was for centuries entrusted to the Overseers of the Poor, elected annually. The task was no easy one, for while seeking to alleviate genuine hardship, the funds to achieve this had to come from the parishioners. They expected the Overseers

*Thomas Scalis, a priest serving Shaftesbury Abbey in 1532, who was 'kind and generous to the poor'.*

to ensure that no unqualified persons received relief – even to the extent of getting them legally evicted from the parish.

As one example, under the heading 'Removal of a Poor Person' The village Vestry Meeting Minutes recorded in 1894 that: 'In 1893 Robert Ramsey was moved from Knoyle to Hindon, he came back and was removed again. In 1894 he returned to Knoyle and was sent to West Knoyle, where he remained'.

Assisted emigration to Canada and the USA was a means employed in the 1830s and 1840s to terminate calls on Parish funds, or put more optimistically, to enable the emigrants to make a fresh start. In 1835, a rate was made to collect £40 so that Luke Fletcher, his wife and four children could emigrate – and the Poor Law Commissioners were asked to contribute money. Whether the appeal was successful is not clear, but in the same year the Churchwardens of East Knoyle were authorised, in conjunction with Mr Candy, to borrow from any Bank – or other source – a sufficient sum of money, that with Mr Seymour (of Knoyle House) having provided £60, could be used to pay the expenses of sending suitable people to America.

In 1842, one year after the Workhouse and Public Cottages were sold by auction, and the property turned into a Farm House (Park Farm); the Parish Overseers of the Poor applied again to the Poor Law Commissioners for money to pay off a debt incurred in 'emigrating certain poor persons from East Knoyle'. They applied again the following year, so that Thomas Matthews, his wife and family could be sent to Canada.

There were also authorised collections in churches for disaster relief, and sometimes for the support of neighbouring parishes in distress . . . which could breed considerable dissension!

One such issue arose in 1831 and 1832; when two local Justices of the Peace ordered the East Knoyle Vestry to provide money to help the poor of neighbouring Hindon. It was decided at a Vestry Meeting on 30 December 1831 to appeal against the Order, and to dispute the same until the next General Quarter Sessions.

In the matter of individual private benevolence; with the upheaval following the Reformation, interfactional rivalry between the old Catholic religion and the new Church of England was rife. The latter was itself ravaged by the struggle between traditional and puritan influences, and finally the English Civil War produced a climate in which charitable benevolence by private individuals was slow to grow.

However, by his will of August the 15th 1687, Robert Compton was to lead the way in East Knoyle. He had farmed Chapel Farm, in the north of the parish, which had been leased to him by the Lord of the Manor. Since 1204, this lordship had been in the hands of the Bishops of Winchester, and was retained by them until Victorian times when that role was assumed by the 'Ecclesiastical Commissioners' of the Church of England, since 1948 known as the 'Church Commissioners'. They still assert that right. However, in the middle of the 20th Century, the late Lady Cunningham's father, Mr Jefferys of Little Leigh, purchased the Common Lands of East Knoyle from them. He kept the windmill, but gave the lands to East Knoyle Parish Council.

Mr Compton gave £300, to be invested in land for the purposes of binding orphan children as apprentices and to relieve the 'old and feeble poor', not receiving any other relief. He also set up the Rector (the Reverend Richard Hill) and a number of trustees to administer his bequest, which remains the basis of the East Knoyle charity today. Three years after her husband died his widow bought a further eleven acres at Moors Farm to benefit the parish's unrelieved poor. If allowance is made for the modernising of the calendar, this was paid out at about the time of the Berwick Hill Fair, which was held behind Berwick St. Leonard, and the payment used to be known as Berwick Fair Money This was probably because the first administrator of widow (Susanna)'s charity was Sir James Howe of Berwick St. Leonard.

Susanna's parcel of land was for many years rented out to the occupiers of Moors Farm, which at one time belonged to the Duchy of Cornwall. At some point after the Caddy family bought the farm from the Duchy, they approached the Charity and asked to buy it. Since it could not be rented out to anyone else, because of the access to it, the Charity agreed in or about 1956.

At some stage two other benefactors, Francis Morley and Edward Sanger, created subsidiary charities.

With the pattern set, other bequests followed. The Reverend Charles Trippett, Rector in 1707, set up a charity under his Will to be administered by Mr Compton's Trustees. This was to be 'put out at Interest and the Interest employed for a School for the poor Children of East Knoyle'. Highly regarded in the parish, he was buried in the chancel, close to the altar. It was no doubt expected that his commemorative tablet would remain there for ever. However, this came to naught during the church restoration of 1876, for when the chancel was refloored, the five memorial tablets in the floor were removed and brass initials were supposed to be inserted in the new floor. Only two, of which Mr. Trippett was one, were in fact placed in position; with all the stones now lying under the second churchyard yew tree, against the wall of Church Cottage.

*The gravestone of Parish benefactor the Reverend Charles Trippett.*

Another benefactor was the Rector in 1745, the Reverend John Shaw. He gave £50 to benefit the poor, later augmented by his widow Mary.

Anthony Burbidge bequeathed £100 in his will to relieve poor widows and widowers over 50. However, anyone receiving this bounty was required to go the parish church 'and there receive, if not sick, the Holy Sacrament at least once a year'. He also gave £20 to set up a Sunday School.

A relatively modern charity that brought great benefits to orphans and other vulnerable children was the Beatrix Nursery, located at Clouds House. This was

*The Beatrix Nursery.*

named after the Dowager Lady Pembroke of Knoyle House. It was established as a Children's Society Home, and it was a remarkably happy and successful institution.

Under the benevolent direction of 'Matron' (Miss Ada Blake) and 'Sister' Miss Guendolen Wilkinson, with a dedicated team of Children's Nurses and support staff, the Home flourished for over 20 years from November 1943. Many of the children, long since grown up returned to the village over the years to seek out Miss Blake, Miss Wilkinson and former nurses, some of whom still live locally.

One such was John Youles, the son of Mrs. Frances Godfrey. Family circumstances were such that it was felt that the best way to provide a good home and parental affection would be through adoption. In the short term however, the Children's Society were approached and agreed to place the child with the Beatrix Nursery, which he joined on the 9th of September 1946. In all probability he was welcomed into the 15 baby unit known as 'Snowdrop' – in Clouds drawing room. The unit had 'en suite' facilities with an array of basins for bathing the infants.

Mr and Mrs Youles of Ilford in Essex who had applied to adopt a child once before, did so again – this time successfully. After the laid down three month trial period, the baby joined the Youles family at the start of a happy childhood. He changed his name to John Youles, and after a full career in the Regular Army, retired with the rank of Captain. He now devotes a lot of his time to the regimental affairs of the Royal Anglian Regiment and its former parts, especially the Essex Regiment.

The Parish Charity Book records make interesting reading over the years, and show that the Trustees discharged their duties conscientiously. They took care to see that the Charity Fields were properly maintained. Occasionally, tenants of Charity Lands sought to reduce the rental to be paid. One notable example occurred in 1886, when agriculture was in a depressed state. In that year the Honourable

*Captain John Youles at East Knoyle in 2007. As a very small boy he had briefly been in the care of Miss Blake and Miss Wilkinson at the Beatrix Nursery.*

Percy Wyndham, who had bought the Clouds House site from Alfred Seymour of Knoyle House and had had a new mansion constructed, was relying on agricultural rents from the tenants of his eleven farms to make a substantial contribution to the upkeep of his estate. Unfortunately, agriculture was suffering from a severe and longlasting depression – brought about by poor harvests and the low price of cheap imported grain. Mr Wyndham found himself in some difficulty, and so wrote to the Trustees asking for a reduction of 15% in the rent which he was paying for Charity Land because he had been 'obliged to make large reductions to his tenants' in 'the present state of agricultural matters'. The Trustees agreed. In August 1897 Mr Wyndham resigned as a Trustee and the agent for the Seymour Estate, Mr Charles Russell of Prospect House was appointed in his stead. He lived in a substantial house built for him in 1867 in Shaftesbury Lane by Alfred Seymour – the stone plaque on the house bears his initials and the date.

In the Minutes of the Charity Book for 1864, the Trustees recorded the state of King's Cottage in Upton in the north of the parish, which they owned, and from which the rent went into the Charity account. Robert King had been the tenant for many years, living there with his wife Louisa and their three children and paying £3 a year in rent. When he died in 1850, his widow remained in occupation until her own death ten years later

In 1853, with the property in disrepair, remedial measures were put in hand. George Elliott, who lived on Charity land at Hangwood Ground (paying £14.17 rent a year), provided straw at a cost of One Pound eleven shillings (£1.55p), Arthur Feltham did the thatching for nine shillings and three pence (46p), George Ricketts the carpenter charged nine shillings and tuppence (46p) and Job Brockway the mason sent in a bill for three shillings and sixpence (17.5p). In the next year, the Trustees took out an insurance policy on the cottage. During the ten years from 1853 to 1862, repairs cost the Charity £25 -6-6 (£25.32p) while the rent produced just £30. In 1864, the Trustees recorded: 'there is no rent from the cottage, it having burnt down'. They added that the insurance company had paid out £85-10-0 (£85.50) which had been invested in an annuity that each year brought in £2-16-4 (£2.82) and from then onwards there was no insurance or repairs to pay for and the cottage garden was let for 15 shillings (75p) a year.

In 1975, the Charity Commissioners introduced a revised scheme tidying up the village charities. They now consist of just two Trusts: Robert and Susan Compton's and Dr. John Shaw's – under the title of The East Knoyle Welfare Trust; with the Revd Trippett's and Mary Shaw's under the title of the East Knoyle Educational Charity.

In 2007, income from land rental, dividend receipts and bank interest amounted to £1877.97. There were 20 applicants for relief presented to the Trustees at their annual meeting at Whitsuntide. Payments were made either as a cash contribution to meet bills for electricity or heating oil, or by a delivery of solid fuel to people's homes. A sum was kept in case of emergency requests for help during the winter months. In previous years help had been given to help apprentices or students with money to buy such items as books or tools – but in 2007 no young persons applied under that heading.

It is good that the benevolence of donors three hundred years ago is still providing significant relief in the 21st Century.

# 'Eat, Drink and be Merry'

I N 2008, Knoyle boasts two inns, one (the Seymour Arms) in Knoyle Street; the other (the Fox and Hounds) run by New Zealander Murray Seator up at The Green.

But that's less than half the story. In 1881 the Fox and Hounds is described as a licensed beer or cider house presided over by Sophia Burton, widow of Isaac with their two daughters. However, its origins may go much further back than that.

*The Fox and Hounds Inn at the Green, 2002.*

An advertisement in the *Salisbury Journal* of 5 July 1784 refers to East Knoyle as 'extremely eligible for a sportsman, being situated on the edge of the Wiltshire Downs, having a pack of harriers kept in the parish, and within four miles of an excellent pack of foxhounds, together with the best partridge, pheasant and woodcock shooting in the kingdom'.

The foxhounds were, and are, the South and West Wilts pack kennelled at Motcombe, but where the harrier pack was is not clear. In 1776, eight years earlier, the Journal advertises an estate for sale at Thomas Williams's at *The Hare and Hounds in East Knoyle* and in 1785 the Journal calls on anyone with information about a missing pony to let Mr Williams know '*at the sign of the Hare and Hounds in East Knoyle*'. It is tempting to speculate that The Hare and Hounds was renamed when the harrier pack disappeared and assumed the title of the nearby foxhound pack which still hunts in the area and would have been familiar to Knoyle inhabitants. A conveyance of 1890 of 'that Messuage or public house known by the name of 'The Fox and Hounds'' makes it clear that this is the property left by John Ricketts to Sarah Jukes for her lifetime in his Will of 22 June 1836. Further research may one day clear things up.

Soon after the turn of the 19th/20th Century The Fox and Hounds was run by the Jukes family, whose son Sidney progressed from Knoyle School to Grammar School and qualifying as a pilot, was commissioned into the Royal Flying Corps – later to become the Royal Air Force. After active service in France he became a flying instructor but was tragically killed in an air accident just at the end of World War I – The Matron and Staff at Plumstead Hospital placed the fine processional cross in St. Mary's Church in his memory.

The Coombes family were the next landlords, handing over to Tom Hall and his wife in 1953. Tom's mother was an East Knoyle girl, and he and his wife Doris (known to the family as 'Doll') soon made their mark. For a start the two seater earth closet at the end of the garden was discarded in favour of indoor sanitation put in by Tom himself.

The life of the pub continued to be quite as busy as under the Coombes. A group of regulars used to come up from the main village on most days, bringing their bread and cheese with them to toast by the fire, while Doris provided the necessary accompaniments of pickled onions, eggs and cabbage. One 'Regular' (George Fletcher) liked his cider mulled and used to take a red hot poker out of the fire to heat it up . . .

Every week Tom took a day off to go sea fishing at Weymouth. The catch, which was usually mackerel, being shared out among family and friends. On one occasion this included an enormous conger eel, duly cooked by Doris, though she doesn't quite remember how she managed it.

The pub ran a notable darts team, as well as a popular skittle alley (still in use) and musical evenings were a regular feature – with the band being a skiffle group with Tom on piano accordion, Bill Campbell on piano, a tea chest and other instruments. On Saturday

*Regular customers at The Fox and Hounds. Tom Hall, the landlord is entertaining them on his piano accordion.*

nights dancing the Twist continued into the early hours. The Fox was reckoned to be the 'in' pub in the area during the swinging 50s and 60s – it even had one of the first televisions in the village, with the children crowding around it on Saturday mornings and the adults watching sport in the afternoon.

Animals were much in evidence. The first was a piglet given by farmer John Jesse soon after they arrived – this animal

*(top left) Tom Hall's giant conger eel, caught at Weymouth and cooked by his wife Doris. (above) The piglet, presented to Mr. and Mrs. Hall by Mr. John Jesse of Chapel Farm. (left) Mrs. Hall and 'Bambi'.*

spent its first few weeks in the stock room until big enough to move into its pigsty. There was also a pony called 'Knocky Bill' (nobody seems to know why), Judy the border collie, geese, a parrot, budgies, a couple of squirrels and a tiny orphaned deer found by Tom and Doris' son. It was brought up in the pub and, not surprisingly it was called 'Bambi'.

The Halls retired in 1977. Doris still lives locally in Gillingham and the pub is now owned by Mr Andrew Knight.

The foundations of the Seymour Arms in The Street rest on the line of the Roman road which ran from Badbury Rings to Bath, with the present buildings dating from the 16th to the 19th centuries. It takes its name from the branch of the Seymour family that owned Knoyle House (now demolished) from at least the 18th century until 1954.

At one time however, it was known as the Benett Arms after the family at Pythouse just over a mile away towards Tisbury. Pythouse was the scene of the so-

*The Seymour Arms, once the Benett Arms, but renamed after Mr. Alfred Seymour had built up his estate in the village to become the principal landowner.*

called Battle of Pythouse in 1830 when John Benett MP called in the Hindon Troop of the Yeomanry to subdue several hundred rioters. In a Victorian example of 'political correctness' the name was changed as Henry and later Alfred Seymour built up the Knoyle Seymours' estate to be the largest in the area, at one time comprising well over half the village.

Both Alfred and Henry Danby Seymour were local MPs, moving spirits in driving through the railway from Salisbury to Yeovil (the first turf being ceremonially cut at Gillingham in 1857 with the silver cased wheelbarrow used now displayed in the Gillingham Museum) and the line opened for traffic two years later.

Thomas and later Henry Ball were the licensees for at least 30 years from 1848,while by 1889 under Charles King, the establishment proclaimed itself as an hotel, wine and spirit merchant and posting house (within easy collection distance by pony and trap of Semley station). Mr Samson was the licensee in the 1930's when the inn belonged to the quaintly named People's Refreshment House Association Ltd. It is now a Wadworth's house.

Also in Knoyle Street used to be The Black Horse with one inn sign inside, probably painted by an itinerant artist in return for beer and something to eat. Another was affixed to the wall just under the eaves.

*An inn sign for the Black Horse, probably executed by an itinerant artist in return for food and drink (reproduced by courtesy of Mr. Andrew Burton).*

*The former Black Horse Inn in The Street.*

We know that a freehold estate was auctioned there in 1767, and a 'horse to cover' two years later, while timber was auctioned ten days before Christmas in 1777. The inn was the Headquarters of the Wiltshire Friendly Society, providing a very worthwhile sickness benefit scheme for a small weekly contribution. Every year, after Whitsun there was a colourful parade of members behind the Knoyle Band , with a church service (packed out, since those attending receiving a payment!) followed by a celebration dinner. The Society lasted for over a hundred years from 1810, not being formally wound up until 1929. Thirza Compton was the licensee in 1848, followed by Daniel Barnard who was also a brewer and horsebreaker, James Spong and Richard Drake (the Drakes are still a farming family in the parish). Daniel Barnard presumably sold his own beer, but there were a number of other local beer retailers around over the years. About the same time (in 1848) James Getley was one, as was Sarah Jukes, whose family later took over the Fox and Hounds. Isaac Burton at the same establishment is also recorded as brewing his own beer. Finally, Mrs Nancy Sanger, who farmed in West Knoyle in the 1850s, was in the business too.

There is a mention in the *Salisbury Journal* of a fourth inn in the parish, called 'The George' where some premises were sold by auction in March 1781 but until recently this seemed to have sunk without trace. However, 'Steeple Close' in Milton at the bottom of the hill opposite 'The Homestead' which was once the home of the blacksmith with his forge nearby, now seems to be a possible candidate. Milton was, and is, the second largest settlement in the parish. The

*'Steeple Close', possible site of the former George Inn (from a watercolour by the late Mrs. Susan Scammell).*

layout of the property with a substantial cellar, and its position close to the farrier's shop – where a thirst might well need quenching during shoeing operations – and its apparent age, all argue in its favour.

Many farms in the West Country used to brew cider for the family and farm

*'The Homestead', once home to the Milton blacksmiths and formerly containing a brewhouse.*

workers until quite recent times, and as already mentioned there was a brewhouse in The Homestead, an 18th century smallholding and now a private house in the hamlet of Milton. The roof trusses could go back to the 16th Century, being the remains of a timber framed house later rebuilt in brick and stone. The brewhouse portion of the property is mid 19th Century, with its typical brick stack and square opening, while the high unceiled room would have helped to dissipate the heat. The house was formerly called 'Marshall's', and Henry Marshall's will of 1599 survives. He was the blacksmith mentioned above, and he and his son Robert died in quick succession, suggesting that this may have been from an infection. The blacksmith's shop a few yards down the hill, survived in Milton into the 20th Century.

There was a cidermaking farm in the next village of West Knoyle which used to attract regulars at weekends, and it is said that at least one of these entered the farm on the Saturday and was not seen again until Monday.

When the author came to Knoyle thirty years ago it was still possible to buy cider from this farm. It was very sweet tasting on the day of purchase, but seemed to get rather rough if kept longer.

By the late 19th century, drunkenness had become recognised as a major social evil, especially amongst the poorer sections of the community; not only because of the dire effects it could have on the health of working men, but also because of the misery and even violence inflicted on their families. All too often, mother would be struggling to bring up the children on what was left of the breadwinner's already low wages after drink had taken its toll.

In Knoyle, the Rector, Canon Milford, was well aware of the situation, and did something about it by starting a branch of the Church of England Temperance Society. With adult and junior sections, this held regular meetings, occasionally with barracking – which the Rector was well able to contain – where visiting speakers gave vivid examples of the ravages of alcohol, and adult members were encouraged to go one step further and to sign a pledge of total abstinence.

The Rector knew however that exhortation and doom-laden warnings would not be effective on their own, so he organised a lively social programme, which was very successful.

On one occasion on July the 26th 1887, the Society ran an outing for 70 members over 14 to the lake at Shearwater 12 miles away. Leaving at midday, the party travelled in five farm wagons, arriving two and a quarter hours later. Two boats had been hired on the lake and many of the members who had never held an oar received instruction in the art of rowing and were said to 'have made great progress'. Tea followed in the boathouse (taken in two relays) where 'great piles of cake and bread and butter' disappeared. After more rowing and a visit to the view from Heaven's Gate, the party set off home, when came 'the only mishap of the day, namely very heavy rain (the first rain for many weeks) which came down steadily and lasted (though with less violence) during most of the drive home. However Temperance people are known to be fond of water and the great good humour and absence of grumbling among the members was noticeable'.

# Snapshots of Knoyle in 1937 and during World War II

I N RECENT YEARS, our villages have seen many, many changes in property ownership and social makeup, and not least in the move from relative self sufficiency to supermarket culture and shopping on the internet.

Some of these, evident in the decline in the local shops and services, are shown in the following 'snapshots'. Of course in 1937 we were in the coronation Year of King George VI, propelled to the throne by the abdication in December 1936 of his elder brother David, due to be crowned King Edward VIII, who gave up his throne rather than abandon his relationship with the American divorcee Mrs 'Wally' Simpson.

While there was a good range of cameras available to serious photographers, for many families the recorder of family events was the Kodak Box Brownie camera. Inexpensive and simple to operate – so long as you mastered the technique of holding the camera steady and avoided fast moving subjects – the results if properly developed and printed would last a lifetime. Some of the illustrations in this chapter were taken on such a camera.

## The Village in 1937

K NOYLE HOUSE, the historic home of a branch of the Seymour family for over two centuries was legally the property of Miss Jane Margaret Seymour. Born in 1874, in her early years she was friendly with Rector Milford's daughters, although Violet writing in her diary in 1892 seems to have found her slightly odd. Sadly, this developed into a mental illness which meant that she was cared for in a nursing home on the south coast until her death at the age of 69. The affairs of the estate were placed in the hands of a family trust and administered through Messrs Rawlence & Squarey of Salisbury, to whom rents and water rates were paid.

Knoyle House was let to tenants. For some thirty years the lease was held by the Dowager Countess of Pembroke, who took an enduring interest in the village and the welfare of its people. She was the much-loved Founding President of the East Knoyle Branch of the Women's Institute, with the Rector's wife, Mrs Cross the Chairman. The Branch was an active one, with over 60 members.

The Mothers' Union (M.U.), originally known as 'The Women's Union' had been founded as a Church of England organisation by Mary Sumner in 1876 with the aim of strengthening and preserving marriage through Christianity. The East Knoyle Branch was the first in Salisbury Diocese, being founded by Mrs Sumner's niece, a daughter of the Rector, Canon Milford, in 1888. A 'trailer' for the new initiative was provided by the Rector in the January 1888 edition of 'The East Knoyle Parish Magazine'. Not exactly billed as headline news, the item was placed after a report of Mr Duprez, 'a well known Conjurer' being engaged by Mrs Seymour to give 'a capital exhibition of conjuring to a large and appreciative audience' the proceeds of which, amounting to more than £3, were given towards a fund for buying a school piano.

In the next paragraph, the Rector gave notice of a forthcoming meeting to consider starting a Branch of the Women's Union. There would be a tea, followed by a short meeting . . . 'All women, of all classes, in the parish would be invited to it'. Fifty years later, the Branch Golden Jubilee was celebrated which was a successful occasion, followed ten years later by the Diamond Jubilee, when the Deanery M.U. Festival was held in the village. Some 200 members from parishes in the Deanery moved in procession behind their banners to the Festival Service in St. Mary's, at which the Bishop of Salisbury preached 'a memorable sermon' on 'Home'. At the celebration tea afterwards, a 'magnificent cake was cut, to which all the East Knoyle members had contributed ingredients'. A link with the Branch founder was demonstrated by the presence of Mrs Violet Bradby, youngest daughter of Canon Milford and his wife (nee Sumner) , whose 'Thank you' letter to Mrs Cross made it very clear how much she had enjoyed coming back to the village of her childhood.

By 1966, the average number at regular monthly meetings was down to under a dozen, although there was a good attendance at combined meetings with the Congregational Women's Guild from their chapel in The Street. In December the Enrolling Member Mrs Palmer, the Rector's wife, opened a discussion on the future for the MU branch 'in view of declining numbers and failing interest'. It was resolved that after 78 years the Branch should be declared in abeyance. However, it was also decided that it should become an open group to be known as St. Mary's Guild. Forty one years on, the Guild is very much alive, welcoming members from different church backgrounds.

On May the 12th 1937, Coronation Day, every child in the school was presented with a spoon. At 11.45 a.m. a commemorative oak tree was planted in the Memorial Garden by Lady Pembroke, with the whole school present, all 70 or so children helping to fill in the hole with one spadeful of earth each.

Also living in Knoyle House was Lady Pembroke's son Sir George Herbert and her granddaughters Guendolen and Phyllis Wilkinson.

A stone's throw down the road from Knoyle House at No. 16 The Street, Mr Fry sold cigarettes and tobacco and was a shoemaker. There were three cobblers as well: Mr Jimmie Ovens in The Street, who was in Mrs Myrtle Burton's words ' quite a character' and Mr 'Tabby' Street a quarter of a mile away in Holloway, close to yet another cobbler, Mr Doggrell. There was another tobacconist – with a difference – at Franklin House, also in The Street. Mr Young sold herb cigarettes and tobacco to be mixed half and half with the regular stuff.

*Mr. Ernest (Ernie) Mallett's workshop in The Street in the 1930s.*

Ernie Mallett, whose father had been estate carpenter and Clerk of Works at Clouds, ran an undertaker's and ironmongery business from his workshop where Mallett's Close is now. He sold paper, paint, nails and much else besides.

There was a 'picnic shop' in May Cottage, still on The Street, run by Miss Glennie and Miss Hughes, where they baked to order. There was also a café, known as The Bothy, among the buildings of Knoyle House. This was run by Mr Brooks, from whom everyone used to order their Christmas cakes. During the 1939-45 War it was also the Headquarters of the Home Guard Platoon, and one of two Women's Land Army hostels.

Moving up the hill to Holloway, there was Halletts the builders, whose men were true craftsmen – although the firm's office system would not have suited the computer age. The property is now a private house.

Milton, which as already mentioned is the village's second largest settlement, was home at No. 115 to Mr and Mrs Sam Matthews. Mr Matthews had charge of the sheep at Sheephouse Farm on the way to Hindon and was out at work all day. His partially sighted wife who had once been a cook at The Rectory, was a cheerful soul who kept a sweet and tobacco shop. Her response to a greeting was always 'Help yourself' and customers used to put their money in a tin. Only once was there an occasion when her trust was misplaced. Sam discovered the shortfall when he cashed up at the end of the day, unmasked the culprit, and left him a shamed and much chastened man.

There was a flower show each August, held in Broadmead, the field below Knoyle House. Sir Geoffrey Fison allowed his tennis court at the former rectory to be used by the Tennis Club. Whist drives and dances in the Village Hall were very popular. Mrs Hyde (then Mrs Bartlett) ran a Brownie pack. Of course the village had its resident policeman in the person of Mr Beard, later to be honoured as a recipient of Maundy Money from The Queen when she conducted the ceremony at Salisbury.

Mr Barnes was nearly half way through his 38 year stint as Headmaster, with Miss Read and Miss Beagarie as assistant teachers – at that time children stayed on until the age of 14.

There were daily buses to Shaftesbury and Salisbury. The butcher called twice a week, as did the fish man. On Wednesdays, Kenwood's van from six miles away in Gillingham called with everything a pig could supply!

In 2008, there are 12 working farms in the parish, but in 1937 there were rather more, and certainly a much larger workforce. In those days, tractors were in evidence, but horses were still used for much of the heavy work. Until the 1940's the largest farms in the parish, being Knoyle Down Farm, Chapel Farm and Park Farm, had up to some 20 shire horses. Their work including ploughing and pulling the horse drawn reaper binder which cut the corn and bound them into sheaves.

Two horse ploughing (from a pen and ink wash by the late Major Roger Croxton).

A horse reaper binder (from a pen and ink wash by the late Major Roger Croxton).

These were then made up into 'stooks': –a bundle of six or eight sheaves stood up together to dry off before being carried to the rick. This would be set up in a convenient corner, loaded from the farm wagon (fine when the level was low, back breaking when it was high), and then thatched to protect it from the weather until the threshing machine came along. This shuddering piece of equipment was powered by a belt drive from a steam traction engine. Examples of these magnificent iron beasts can be seen each year at the Great Dorset Steam Fair. Nowadays, corn stems are much shorter, but it is still possible to see stooked sheaves where wheat straw is being grown for thatch.

Although recognizably modern milking machines made by Simplex, Alfa-Laval and other manufacturers had been available since before World War I, much of the milking, particularly on farms with smaller herds, was still done by hand. The first milking machine to come to the village was known as a 'milking bail', a movable piece of equipment which could be shifted on skids around the grazing field. Parishioners used to collect their milk from the nearest farm until new laws required all producers selling retail to the public to be registered with the Ministry of Health. This cut down the practice to just three farms, and eventually none. Milk was collected daily from the farms in churns to be transported to the dairy by the milk lorry, which could be heard rattling on its way from quite a distance.

Canon Cross had recently decided to move out of the Rectory at least partly because he reckoned that the ending of the Milk Tithe would reduce his income significantly and make it impossible for him to continue to live there. The house he chose and occupied after months of putting up in the Seymour Arms while building work was completed was a former farmhouse in Holloway close to the sunken lane area. The medieval and Georgian Rectory was renamed 'Knoyle Place' by its new owner Sir Guy Fison. The former farmhouse was a rectory and family home to Canon Cross and to his successor, the Reverend Basil Palmer, until 1975. When he departed, the Diocese sold the house and East Knoyle Parish was combined into a single benefice with Hindon, Chicklade and Pertwood, the last two north of the A303. Confusingly, it then became known as 'The Old Rectory', the name it bears today.

There were quite a number of shops, stores and services. Three general stores competed for business: The Post Office stores in what was formerly the Black Horse Inn, East Knoyle Stores in The Street, run locally, but belonging to Walton's of Mere, and a third run by Mr and Mrs Cochrane at The Green (now 'Four Winds' a private house). Mr Alford was a saddler, next to Forge Cottage in The Street.

*East Knoyle Stores in The Street. On left is Mr. Ernest (Ernie) Francis, brother to Percy, killed during World War II. Mr. and Mrs. Tuck ran the shop. Mr. Stiles Hillier, with his walking stick on the right was a neighbour.*

*Harris' Bakery in The Street in the early 20th Century.*

Harris' bakery (now 'Millbrook'), afterwards Nicholas & Harris operating from Tisbury, delivered bread around the village, as did Avery's over the border in West Knoyle. The latter still do so in 2008, as well as supplying 'Wren's Shop'- to be mentioned later.

If you went into any of these shops and paid by cash, you would have made use of the old Pounds, Shillings and Pence, which remained our currency until decimalization in 1970. In 1937, there were ten coins accepted as legal tender. There was no £2 coin, and no £1 coin either as the Gold sovereign had been withdrawn in 1922, giving way to the Bank of England £1 note. Scottish banks had they own banknotes, as they still do, but in 1937 you were often liable to have sixpence (2.5%) deducted from your change if you presented one! A few sovereigns were and still are minted each year, but there were severe restrictions on holdings by private individuals. Ten shillings (50p) was also supplied as a bank note.

The Crown (25p) coins were still legal tender, but they were only minted on special occasions. The last time this was done was in the Millennium year, when the Royal Mint deployed a small manufacturing unit at the ill-fated Millennium Dome, from which one could buy a specimen.

The largest normal coin was the Half Crown (12.5p). Next in line was the Florin, introduced in 1849 as a silver coin worth two shillings (10p), an early experiment with decimalization. In 1937, the design of the silver 'threepenny-bit' was changed from a figure three with a crown above it to a shield with the cross of St. George on a Tudor rose. At the same time a larger twelve sided nickel-brass threepenny coin was introduced, with a government joke included – the design was a thrift plant, at a time when saving up was being encouraged. The author had a rather smart green metal money box with the Royal Arms and a one way slot. At the end of the holidays this was taken to the village postmaster to be unlocked and the contents credited into a Post Office Savings Account Book. There was no two penny coin, but a large penny one, with Britannia on one side, the sea behind her and a lighthouse. The halfpenny (pronounced 'hayp-nee') changed its design after the death of King George V. The new coin, first seen in public on King George VI's coronation year, carried a sailing ship, said to represent Sir Francis Drake's 'Golden Hind'. It was abolished on decimalization, with the new two pence (2p) piece being just about the same size but valued at almost five times as much . . .

In 1937, there was one more even smaller coin, the farthing – worth a quarter of one (old) penny. It was not often necessary to use one, but bakeries quite often valued their loaves to including farthings, for instance one shilling and elevenpence threefarthings. It was another new design, which was awaiting royal approval when King Edward VIII abdicated in December 1936. In 1937, the little Britannia was replaced with Britain's smallest bird the Wren. Within 20 years the farthing was reckoned to serve no further useful purpose and minting ceased in 1956. The coin ceased to be legal tender on December the 31st 1960.

There was one royal occasion with Knoyle connexions in 1938 which did not make the headlines, nor were any snapshots taken that have survived; although it was reported in 'The Tatler'. HRH Princess Elizabeth (now Queen Elizabeth II) and her younger sister Princess Margaret (more commonly known at that time as 'Princess Margaret Rose') visited Sir Nevile Wilkinson. Sir Nevile was then Ulster King of Arms, one of the senior officers of the College of Arms in London, having held the office since 1908. Since King Edward VIII's abdication in December 1937, he had been a very busy man with state duties preparing for and attending the Coronation of King George VI and Queen Elizabeth, clad in his magnificent 'tabard' or heraldic tunic in red and gold. His salary was, at least until recently, set at under £20, having never been revised since Tudor times. Fortunately, his main work was concerned with grants of (coats of) arms to individuals and public bodies, which was rather more lucrative.

Sir Nevile, father of the late Miss Guendolen Wilkinson, well remembered as 'Sister' at the Beatrix Children's Nursery at Clouds, had a most unusual outside interest. Over a period of 15 years, a skilled painter himself and working with a staff of outstanding craftsmen, he created 'Titania's Palace' ( measuring ten feet by seven feet, with over 3,000 components) lovingly bringing to life his fairy story 'Yvette in Italy', published by Rector Milford's son Humphrey at The Oxford University Press in 1922. This palace was exhibited in many parts of the world, and this is what the two princesses went to see in London, spending a number of happy hours admiring it. Sir Nevile died in 1940, but the palace remained in the family for another 20 years, when it was sold to an English amusement park, and then to Legoland. It is now one of the major attractions at Egeskov Castle, on Southern Funen, also in Denmark.

## World War II

As in the rest of the country, the war saw many of the young people serving in the Forces, of whom twelve were never to return. Their names are inscribed on the Village War Memorial, erected in 1919 after World War I, as well as on a memorial plaque in St. Mary's Church where the Roll of Honour is read out each Remembrance Sunday. Clouds Park became an army camp with huts erected in the grounds, and for a while the Village Hall was requisitioned.

Francis ('Frank') Bolton who now lives with his wife in Connecticut, was one of those growing up in the village in wartime. Born in 1934, he moved to the village with his parents and brothers when he was two years old. His father, also called Frank, worked for Major Houghton Brown, who at that stage was living at Clouds with his family. Father's job was to look after the horses, but he also acted as chauffeur when needed. During the War, the Bolton family lived in the Clouds Stables building and Frank (Junior) went to the village school.

*Frank Bolton with the East Knoyle School group during the May Queen celebrations in 1944 (See Key No. 34).*

He has many pleasant memories of his childhood, describing them as 'some of the happiest years of my life'. He had many friends at school, although he encountered some bullying because he lived in and had connections with Clouds: the 'Big House'.

| | | | | |
|---|---|---|---|---|
| 1 John Parsons | 7 Richard Hyde | 13 Christine Hull | 19 Molly Browning | 25 Janet Tansweil | 31 Jean? |
| 2 Terence? | 8 Grace Hull | 14 Eric Jefford | 20 Betty Fletcher | 26 Diane Tansweil | 32 Susan |
| 3 Stephen Tuck * | 9 Betty? Lynch | 15 Chris Tuck * | 21 Audrey Hughs | 27 Evelyn Fricker | Cochrane |
| 4 Terry Gadsby | 10 Brenda Hull | 16 Janet Tuck* | 22 Gillian Obrien | 28 Violet Hull | 33 Joan Chubb+ |
| 5 Geof Hughs | 11 Janice Tuck | 17 Mary Bartlett | 23 Ivor Browning | 29 Shelia Cochrane | 34 Francis Bolton |
| 6 Margaret Lynch? | 12 Margaret Chubb+ | 18 Kitty Hyde | 24 Gordon Jefford | 30 Jean Conlin? | 35 David Chubb + |
| | | | | | 36 John Scammell |
| | | | | | 37 Robin Butler |

* or + same family

By the road to Sheephouse Farm, Frank remembers playing with other boys in and around the lime kiln, which had ceased working in 1931. One day at the kiln, a boy reached inside one of the pillars and drew out an old sword – which Frank feels may well have dated from the English Civil War. He would dearly have loved to own it, but his negotiations to provide a swap failed – and the sword is no longer available.

Frank (Senior) became friendly with Captain Collier, one of the officers billeted in the grounds of the 'Big House'. They used to talk of the slaughter in the First World War which had ended only a little over twenty years before. The Captain became very depressed with what he saw as an impending repeat of the horrors of 1914-1918. Tragically, he felt impelled to take his own life.

On the outbreak of war in September 1939, the Houghton Browns decided to leave Clouds House, as they felt it would be too expensive to keep up. They rented

Cleeve, a few hundred yards away, and leased Clouds to Miss Chynoweth at an annual rent of £300. Under her direction, Clouds later became home to a secretarial college, with Frank's father acting as caretaker when the college was on holiday. On one occasion Frank was put in charge of handing over the keys of the house to returning members of the college staff. As he waited at the top of the kitchen steps just as it was getting dark, he saw two ladies approaching. He called out a greeting, but was surprised to receive no acknowledgement or reply. The figures continued to walk round the path and down the steps into the garden, talking as they went. His curiosity aroused, Frank now began to follow them and was struck by the fact that they were in Elizabethan dress. As he started down the steps after them, they quite suddenly disappeared. Although Frank would not have known it at the time, Thomas Cloud (or Clowde) occupied an earlier house on the site in 1581, in Queen Elizabeth the First's reign. To this day, over 60 years later, the memory remains in Frank's mind as vividly as ever.

After the military were in residence, soldiers in the hutted camp reported hearing the sound of horses and carriage wheels from the drive leading south towards Slades just outside the park. The sounds appeared so real that one soldier on guard is reported to have cried out in fright and fainted to the ground. These reported happenings were only experienced by the British troops – never by the Americans of the 3rd (US) Spearhead Division training for the invasion of Normandy in 1944.

Sadly, Frank's brother William was killed in 1940, shortly before his friend Alastair Houghton Brown. Both names appear on the village war memorials. Frank's son, who came to visit Knoyle with his father was named Alastair after his great friend, whose memory is kept alive by the memorial board on the stage of the Village Hall given by the Houghton Brown family in Alastair's memory.

Frank moved with his family to Eastbourne when he was about 13, and he went to Eastbourne Grammar School. He was not happy there, and spent many hours wondering how he could escape and run back to his beloved Knoyle.

In Connecticut, where Frank now lives, he manages his wife's equestrian establishment.

### A Postscript – Richard Ricketts' Fight against Bureaucracy

THE YEARS AFTER the end of World War II saw the birth of the Welfare State; with the introduction of the National Health Service and a wide range of benefits under Social Security legislation. However, success in claiming them under the complex regulations can sometimes be both frustrating and time-consuming.

This is no new phenomenon, as Richard Ricketts found out 350 years ago during the English Civil War. In 1646, the English Civil War was at its height. Families were torn apart, with fathers and their sons sometimes passionately at odds. However for many, especially in the countryside, it was a case of 'A plague on both your houses – leave us alone to get on with our lives'.

Such apparently was the opinion of Richard, a member of the large local Ricketts family which included prosperous farmers, farm labourers, sawyers and gardeners. He claimed that he was pressed into Royalist service and carried into Longford garrison near Salisbury commanded by Sir Jonathan Pell. In the subsequent fighting he was 'dangerously wounded and crippled'. He then petitioned the Parliamentary authorities for compensation, and to back him up presented a memorial signed by numerous inhabitants of Knoyle, headed by the Rector and Dean of Windsor, Dr Christopher Wren, father of the architect of St. Paul's cathedral. His petition was postponed, but Mr Ricketts was not to be so easily put off. He petitioned again in January 1646/7, but this time the memorial was refused outright being marked 'Noe order'. A third appeal on January the 3rd 1647/8 was thrown out once more, marked 'Null fact'. Nevertheless the Quarter Sessions later granted him an order for one shilling and sixpence (7.5p) weekly, though in July 1649 he complained that he hadn't been paid for four weeks. By this time he had clearly become disenchanted with authority, to put it mildly; for in 1650 he was reported as being 'profane, a drunkard, and of very ill behaviour'.

# 'Staying Postal'
# Knoyle's Royal Mail

THE RECORDED HISTORY of the village's postal service goes back over a hundred and forty five years, and pride of place must go to successive generations of the Burton family who served the village as postmasters and shopkeepers until retiring in 1968.

Samuel Burton, born in Tisbury, was appointed Sub Postmaster in 1862 at the age of 32, and lived with his wife Eliza and their family in a house close to The Square, which was pulled down in the late 1880s. This event was duly recorded in two watercolours by Jane Bouverie, a member of the Seymour family living in Knoyle House nearby.

He must have quickly established himself, for three years later he was recorded in the 1865 edition of 'Harrod's Directory' as one of the 'Chief Inhabitants of East Knoyle – Grocer and Postmaster'.

The running of the Post Office and the grocery shop was clearly a family affair. At the 1881 Census, sons Henry and William are

*The Burton family home on the corner of The Square (where the War Memorial now Stands) being demolished in the late 1880s (from a watercolour by Jane Bouverie of Knoyle House opposite).*

both described as 'Letter Carriers'. Ten years later Henry had become a 'Grocer's assistant' and young daughter Annie was employed as 'Postmaster's Clerk'.

*The Post Office in 1942, in part of the former Black Horse Inn building.*

After the Burtons' house had been demolished, the Post Office moved to Black Horse House, which had ceased to be an inn. Henry Burton succeeded his father as Postmaster at the turn of the 19th/20th Century.

Military manoeuvres used to be held periodically at Summerleaze, and provided a spectacle for eager onlookers. They also created a lot of extra work for the Knoyle Postmaster and his staff. It is pleasing to note that on at least one occasion this was rewarded with a formal commendation. Addressed to 'Mr. Burton, East Knoyle' and dated 9 November 1898, it read:

'The Postmaster General has had before him reports from the officer who superintended the Telegraph arrangements in connection with the recent Military Manoeuvres.

The work thrown upon the officers of the Department during these Manoeuvres was disposed of both promptly and accurately although it was not only extremely heavy but had to be dealt with under very disadvantageous conditions.

His Grace has read the reports on the subject with much pleasure and interest, and he wishes that the Postmaster, Sub Postmaster and Staff concerned in bringing about this satisfactory result should be warmly commended.'

When Henry took over the position from his father, the contract sent for signature from the Acting Postmaster at Salisbury was stern and comprehensive in its detail. He had to be a householder, 'not connected with any Inn or Public House'. He was specifically barred from a long list of employments. Some of these were obvious but included were work as Station Master, Overseer of the Poor, Vaccination Officer, Money Lender, or 'any other business which the Department will require you to perform for itself.'

He had to have 'East Knoyle Post Office'in large letters outside the office – and this survived as a black lettered enamel notice until the last days of Mr Atrill's appointment in 2004.

Arrangements for the layout were precise – 'the properly constructed letter box' for instance, 'must be in a wall or window, and not in a door'. But most onerous, perhaps, was the requirement to give 'Bond to the Postmaster General in the sum of £200' – A very substantial sum indeed in those days – through one of several approved Guarantee Societies.

In 1898 Henry married Elizabeth Orchard who was Mrs Seymour's Lady's Maid at Knoyle House, and the family still own the wedding dress – which was exhibited at the 'Festival of Marriage' held in the church in 1991. In the modern business jargon, Henry also 'diversified'. He obviously got round the employment restrictions; for he ran a hackney carriage service – going to Semley station up to eleven times a day.

Henry and Elizabeth's first son was William Henry (known as 'Bill') who was born in Black Horse House on June the 10th 1900. William went into partnership with his brother-in-law Albert Sully who married Henry's daughter Gladys, who also worked in the Post Office. Albert was later to become the blacksmith in 1922 at the forge in The Street. In 1937 William moved to Upper Leigh Farm, living there until 1965, when he and his wife Emily occupied the bungalow in Leigh Lane nearby. After that the couple moved to Shaftesbury, where they celebrated their Diamond Wedding in 1986.

Another of Henry's sons was Clifford, who entered the village record books in 1931 as the winner of the first Village Hall Billiard Competition, held in what is still known as the 'Billiard Room'. The prize for this was a handsome cased billiard cue. Six years later, on the occasion of his marriage to Myrtle, he was appointed Sub Postmaster in succession to his father. During World War II, when Clifford was serving overseas with the Royal Wiltshire Yeomanry, Myrtle combined bringing up her six children with the business of running the Post Office in place of her husband. One of her responsibilities, sometimes a sad one, was to deliver telegrams to Clouds House where in 1943/44 the Americans were preparing for the invasion of Normandy. Although diminutive in size, she was not in the business of being intimidated by authority, proving more than a match for the military on the rare occasions when they tried to interfere with her duty!

Mr Edward (Ted) Burton son of 'Bill' who farmed at Upper Leigh for many years and now lives in Shaftesbury, recalls being paid sixpence (2.5p) to deliver telegrams. One generation down, Mr Andrew Burton remembers being paid a shilling (5p) for doing the same thing, but involving a seven mile round cycle trip up hill and down dale over to Pertwood, north of the A303 – money well earned!

After Clifford retired in 1969, he and Myrtle continued to play an active part in the life of the Congregational Chapel, later amalgamating to become the United Reformed Church (URC), and of the village. Clifford died in 1978. When the URC chapel closed in 1986 on the retirement of Pastor Edith Young, Myrtle accepted an invitation to become a member of St. Mary's Parochial Church Council. In 1993, when the village archive was being put together, Myrtle was one of those who provided much rich material, in her case from experience going back over half a century.

As a youngster, Myrtle was a keen horsewoman and tennis player. Trained as a poultry keeper, she was a champion butter maker and a keen member of the Wiltshire Association of Dairy Students. She liked to go to dances too.

An initiative of the Sunday School under her daughter Christine's leadership was in giving a Christmas Party to elderly village residents; which led to the formation of the 'Good Companions Club' for the over 60's. This ran very successfully for 21 years.

Looking back, it is quite hard to see how she fitted everything into her life. In addition to the activities already mentioned, she was the last President of the Women's Institute in East Knoyle before it was revived in the 1990's. She organised flower shows (at which her Pelargoniums and African Violets were famous) and served on both the Parish Council and the Village Hall Committee. She supported the British Red Cross Society for many years and was a member of the Women's Section of the Royal British Legion.

A Thanksgiving Service for her life was held in St. Mary's Church on 12 May 2006. This was conducted jointly by the Reverend June Lane, Curate of the parish during an interregnum; and the Reverend Julian Thomas, Minister of Salisbury United Reformed Church.

The Burtons' retirement from the Post Office was the end of an era, but not of the story of the Post Office. Over the next 35 years, its fortunes fluctuated. At one stage Mr and Mrs Stamp planned to run the Post Office and shop. Unfortunately, Mr Stamp became ill, so that the postal side was run by staff coming out from Salisbury. Mr John Evans, who had once farmed sheep in Australia, was the next Postmaster, while his wife Beryl ran the shop. They were followed by two former air pilots. The first was Mr Carl Robinson who had been in the RAF while his wife Pam ran the shop until, sadly, she fell a victim to cancer. Their places were taken by Mr Martyn Atrill, formerly in the Fleet Air Arm with his wife – always known as 'Lon'. During their time the stock was run down and Post Office reduced; until closure came in January 2004 when the owners retired.

At this point village retail services were down to one garage with its small but valued shop, a milk delivery round and a traditional baker next door in West Knoyle.

Happily, the village rose to the challenge. After casting around at other possibilities, a proposal to reopen with a new building on Parish Council land next to the War Memorial attracted wide support. People from all sections of the community came forward to offer time, money and all sorts of expertise.

A solid achievement in fundraising, accumulating know-how on ways and means, goodwill from Parish, District and County Councils and finally real support from Mr Jim Knight (then the Rural Affairs Minister) brought forth a substantial grant from the Department for the Environment, Food and Rural Affairs (DEFRA), so that work could begin.

Working to plans from our retired architect Mr Geoff Cook, our village builders Burfitt & Garrett created a sympathetic, practical building using stone from the old bus shelter. It only remained for young admirers of the author Terry Pratchett, whose latest work was then the best seller 'Going Postal' to suggest that he perform the opening ceremony – an invitation which he willingly accepted. The deed was done on 5 August 2006.

In its first full year of operation the entirely volunteer-run shop had a turnover of over £200,000. There was an anxious time when the Post Office authorities announced the intended closure of 2,500 offices throughout the country, with no apparent concern by the Post Office or Government for the negative effects on the

*Mr. Terry Pratchett, the best- selling author of fantasy novels, formally opens Wren's Shop and Post Office on 5 August 2006. At the time his most recently published book was 'Going Postal' – so the author came dressed appropriately!*

wellbeing of rural communities which closure of their post office would have – depriving them of a vital focal point, bringing all sections of the population together.

To have lost the post office would have made the survival of the village shop much more problematic and be a devastating blow to village morale after so much effort to rebuild and reopen after the facility was closed in 2004. Thankfully, although 21 post offices in Wiltshire were marked down for closure, East Knoyle has been spared.

To sum up the theme of this book: For a village community to prosper, a measure of change is right and inevitable. If one were seeking a recipe for successful rural life today, perhaps it might be: 'To aim to preserve a memory of the past, to savour the present and to work –if necessary against the odds – for an enduring future'.

# Notes on Sources

### Castle Rings

1.      Field, Norman, 1992, *Dorset and the Second Legion,* Dorset Books, Tiverton.
2.      Wiltshire County Archaeology Service, The Wiltshire & Swindon History Centre (WSHC).
3.      Dio, Cassius, 229, *Roman History,* Loeb Classical Library.
4.      Avery, Michael, 1993, *Hillfort Defences of Southern Britain,* British Archaeological Reports Series 231.
5.      Benario, H, 2008, *De Imperatoribus Romanis,* Emory University.

### 'Our Daily Bread'

1.      Mr John Reading, East Knoyle, who worked with the author on a fruitful examination of Mill Mead and the course of the mill leat.
2.      Holt, Richard, 1988, *The Mills of Medieval England,* Blackwell, Oxford.
3.      Corfield, M.C. (ed.) 1978, 'East Knoyle Tower Mill Remains', *A Guide to the Industrial Archaeology of Wiltshire,* Wiltshire Library & Museum Service.
4.      Mr Clifford Sully, East Knoyle.
5.      Mr David Pickering, East Knoyle.

### The Admiral and his Lady

1.      The Curator, Archivist and staff of the Teignmouth and Shaldon Museum, who provided much support and access to written sources.
2.      The Admiral's descendant Lieutenant Colonel F.H. Pellew and his daughter Mrs P.G. Jones.
3.      Parkinson, C Northcote, 1934, *Edward Pellew, Viscount Exmouth,* Methuen, London.
4.      Osler, Edward, 1854, *The Life of Admiral Viscount Pellew,* available in hardback at the Teignmouth and Shaldon Museum and online – Project Gutenberg 2006.
5.      Rae, Malcolm, 1999, *Admiral Sir Edward Pellew 1ˢᵗ Viscount Exmouth,* Monograph No. 4, Teignmouth Museum & Historical Society.
6.      Murray, John, 1849, *O'Byrne's Naval Biography,* London (Studied at the Library of the Society of Genealogists).
7.      *Dictionary of National Biography,* 'Edward Pellew', Oxford University Press, 2004.
8.      *Wikipedia 2008,* 'Joseph Antonio Emidy'.
9.      Mr Stafford Clark, local historian of Christow, Devon and of the Pellew connexion.
10.     Mr and Mrs M.S. Cowen, Sedgehill.
11.     Mrs Ruth Drake, Sedgehill.

12. *The Victoria History of Counties of England: Wiltshire,*Volume XIII, 1987, 169-172.

## Knoylian for Ninety Years

1.  Lt Cdr George King RN(Retd), Warsash.
2.  The Honourable Diana Makgill, East Knoyle.
3.  Mrs Winifred Hyde, formerly of East Knoyle.
4.  The Fleet Air Arm Archive.

## A Tale of Two Services – Francis Swain

1.  Lt Col Francis Swain's family papers, with permission from Mrs Sarah Swain.
2.  The Fleet Air Arm Archive.

## Kingston Agate

1.  The Public Records Office, Kew, London – where the ship's record of war service is held.
2.  The Imperial War Museum, London.
3.  Mr Peter Russell Cook, retired Chief Engineer (MN), Colwyn Bay.
4.  Lt Cdr Ivor Howcroft RD* RNR (Retd), Tisbury.
5.  Capt W.W.F. Chatterton Dickson RN (Retd), Tisbury.
6.  The Submariners' Association, Barrow in Furness Branch.
7.  Kingston upon Hull City Council, Leisure Services Department.
8.  Lund, Paul and Ludlam, Harry, 1971, *Trawlers go to War, W Foulsham & Co., London.*
9.  *Hull Daily Mail,* 7 September 1941.
10. *The Times,* 9 September 1941.
11. *Destroyer Photo Index DD-162 USS Thatcher.*
12. *Seedie's Roll of Naval Honours and Awards 1939-1945, Ripley Registers* (Compiled by Capt W.W.F. Chatterton Dickson RN (Retd), Dormer House, Tisbury, Wiltshire).
13. Ashe Lincoln, Commander F, GC RNVR, 1961, *Secret Naval Investigator,* William Kimber, London.
14. Follett, J, *International Maritime Research Database, U571 Lies, Dam Lies, Hollywood!*
15. Costello, J and Hughes, T, 1977, *The Battle of the Atlantic,* Collins, London.

## 'O Praise ye the Lord'

1.  Mr and Mrs Alan Oakley, East Knoyle, owners of the former Ebenezer Chapel, whose meticulous research and support enabled this chapter to be written.
2.  *Faith in Action,* (ISBN 0 906759 45 5) 1988, Cheshire County Council.
3.  Hatcher, Stephen, 1999, *God is building a House* (re: Chapel building, contents and layout), Englesea Brook Chapel and Museum.
4.  Chandler, John  and Parker , Derek, 1993, *The Church in Wiltshire* (re: The spread of Primitive Methodism in Wiltshire ), Hobnob Press, 145-146.
5.  Dolman, Robert, 2007, *Rough Informal Energy: The Story of Primitive Methodism,* Lecture to mark Primitive Methodism's bicentenary, Castle Street Methodist Church, Cambridge, www.castlestreet.org.uk/primitive_methodism.html.

6.    Dorset History Centre (Useful records of Chapel Trustee Meetings and other material).

7.    Mr and Mrs John Lampard and their family (re: Mr Reginald Lampard's long connexion with the life of the East Knoyle Primitive Methodist Chapel), East Knoyle.

8.    Mrs Ruby Jay, East Knoyle.

9.    *Western Gazette,* 12 June and 24 July 1908.

10.    Palmer, Basil, January 1974, *East Knoyle Parish Magazine.*

## Damascus in Knoyle

1.    Mr John Maine RA, the Old School, East Knoyle, whose help and encouragement in the writing of this chapter has been much appreciated.

2.    The East Knoyle Village Archive.

3.    Ms Sabrina Sully, Clerk to the East Knoyle Charity Trustees.

4.    Wiltshire & Swindon History Centre (WSHC), *Charity Commissioners' Reports, Wiltshire 1819-1837;* Report No. 26.

5.    Darby, Elisabeth, 2003, 'Islam in East Knoyle: George Aitchison and the National School 1870-1873'; in *Wiltshire Studies, The Wiltshire Archaeological and Natural History Magazine* (ed. Joshua Pollard, John Chandler and James Thomas), WANHS, 47-53.

6.    *The Victoria History of Counties of England: Wiltshire,* Volume XI, 1980, Institute of Historical Research, University of London. 97-98.

7.    Bradby (nee Milford), Violet, *A Village Chronicle,* Private publication, c1940, 48.

8.    Warburton, William, 1859, *Warburton Census of Wiltshire Schools,* House of Commons.

9.    *Wikipedia* 2008, the Wikimedia Foundation Inc., San Francisco.

10.    Young, Edith, 1984, *The History of East Knoyle School.*

11.    Wiltshire & Swindon History Centre (WSHC), Letters (F8/600/159/1/26/1):
           Milford to Seymour 16 September 1870;
           Milford to Aitchison 3 November 1870;
           Milford to Aitchison 14 November 1870:
           Aitchison to Milford 15 November 1870;
           Seymour to Milford 27 November 1870;
           Aitchison to Milford 15 August 1871;
           Aitchison to Milford 9 May 1872;
           Aitchison to Milford 23 September 1872;
           Aitchison to Milford 30 January 1874.

12.    WSHC F8/500/159/1/1, Tanswell, John, 1863-1882, *East Knoyle School Admissions Register.*

13.    WSHC 186/1, Seymour, A, *Knoyle House Game Book.*

14.    WSHC 1126/16, *Inventory of Knoyle House.*

15.    Falk, Bernard, 1940, *The Naughty Seymours, Hutchinson, 249-255.*

16.    'Laying the Foundation of a New School', *Salisbury & Winchester Journal,* 29 June 1872.

17.    'Opening of a new National School at Knoyle', *ibid,* 7 June 1873.

## Emily

1.    Mrs Julia Brown, Emily's granddaughter, who made available the results of her correspondence with the Children's Society (formerly The Waifs and Strays

Society).
2.      Mr Alan Oakley, East Knoyle (re: The possible location of the Children's Home).
3.      Mrs Jennifer Hynd, East Knoyle.
4.      Mr Clifford Sully, East Knoyle.
5.      The East Knoyle Archive (re: The Milford family involvement).
6.      The Archivist, Powderham Castle, Devon (re: The Kenton Industrial Home).

## Men of Iron

1.      Mr Clifford Sully, East Knoyle.
2.      Mr Michael Hull, East Knoyle.
3.      Mr David Tomlin, East Knoyle.
4.      The East Knoyle Archive (Especially the Women's Institute Scrapbooks).

## The Forgotten Soldier

1.      *The Victoria History of Counties of England, Wiltshire, Volume XIII, 1987*, 71.
2.      The Commonwealth War Graves Commission.
3.      Wiltshire and Swindon History Centre.
4.      Mr Edward Peckham, Hindon.
5.      Mr Eric Price, Burgess Hill. Sussex.
6.      Mr Derek Haighton, Sutton, Surrey (re: Rifle Brigade History in World War I, kindly providing access to: Berkeley, R, *The Rifle Brigade 1914-1918 Volume I 1914-1916)*.
7.      *First World War.com: Battles: The Battle of Guillemont 1916.*

## In Search of a Family

1.      Mr Ernest Francis, now living in Ireland, made contact with the author seeking family information. With the aid of research by Mrs Joan Claydon, and a fruitful visit to Mrs Elizabeth Lampard (nee Francis) both of East Knoyle, a journey of discovery began.

## The Gift of Charity

1.      Chandler, John, 2003, *A Higher Reality,* Hobnob Press.
2.      Ms Sabrina Sully, Clerk to the East Knoyle Charity Trustees.
3.      Wiltshire & Swindon History Centre (WSHC), *Charity Commissioners' Reports, Wiltshire 1819-1837;* Report No. 26.
4.      Steedman, John, 1983, *Wills of Robert Compton, Susanna Compton (re: Berwick Fair Money), Rev Charles Trippett,* Transcripts.
5.      Mickleburgh, R.W., *East Knoyle Charity Book 1697-1869,* Extracts.
6.      Charity Commissioners, *Scheme for East Knoyle Charities,* 134(S) 75, 27 March 1975.
7.      *The Victoria History of Counties of England: Wiltshire,* Volume XI, 1980, Institute of Historical Research, University of London, 97-98.
8.      Stratton, Muriel, *Notes for East Knoyle Women's Institute Scrapbooks,* Volumes I-III, c 1950.
9.      East Knoyle Village Archive, *East Knoyle Women's Institute Scrapbook,* Volume I.
10.     Mr John Youles, who lived in the Beatrix Nursery in 1946.

## Eat, Drink and be Merry

1.     Mrs Doris Hall of Gillingham, whose late husband Mr Tom Hall was landlord of the Fox & Hounds Inn from 1953 to 1977.
2.     Mr Robert Jago, Wiltshire & Swindon History Centre (WSHC), who generously made available his research into Wiltshire inns, with particular reference to information extracted from the *Salisbury Journal*.
3.     Mr Andrew Knight, East Knoyle, present owner of the Fox & Hounds Inn.
4.     *East Knoyle Parish Magazine*, July 1887.
5.     *Kelly's Directory of Wiltshire*, 1939.
6.     *The Wiltshire Buildings Record*, Report on 'The Homestead', Milton.
7.     *The Victoria County History of the Counties of England: Wiltshire*, Volume XI, 1980, 83-85.

## Snapshots of Knoyle: 1937 and World War II

1.     The East Knoyle Village Archive.
2.     Mr Frank Bolton, Connecticut USA.
3.     The late Mrs Myrtle Burton, East Knoyle.
4.     The late Major Roger Croxton, East Knoyle.
5.      Mr Michael Hull, East Knoyle.
6.     The Honourable Diana Makgill, East Knoyle.
7.     Mr Clifford Sully, East Knoyle.

## Staying Postal, Knoyle's Royal Mail

1.     The East Knoyle Village Archive.
2.     The late Mrs Myrtle Burton, East Knoyle.

# Index

Note: References in **bold** are to illustrations.